Holocaust Resistance

Craig E. Blohm

ReferencePoint Press®

San Diego, CA

About the Author

Craig E. Blohm has written numerous books and magazine articles for young readers. He and his wife, Desiree, reside in Tinley Park, Illinois.

For more information, contact:
ReferencePoint Press, Inc.
PO Box 27779
San Diego, CA 92198
www.ReferencePointPress.com

Picture Credits:
Cover: © Hulton-Deutsch Collection/Corbis; Maury Aaseng: 39; Akg-images/Newscom: 11, 42, 47; © Jacek Bednarczyk/epa/Corbis: 32; © Bettmann/Corbis: 19; Everett Collection/Newscom: 8; © Jim Hollander/epa/Corbis: 15; © Reuters/Corbis: 60, 65; Thinkstock Images: 4, 5; © Yonathan Weitzman/Reuters/Corbis: 66; © Kirsty Wigglesworth/AP/Corbis: 51; World History Archive/Newscom: 56; Women in a saddle workshop in the Lodz (Litzmannstadt) ghetto, Lodz, Poland, 1941 (photo), Genewein, Walter (20th century)/© Galerie Bilderwelt/Bridgeman Images: 23; German police arrest Jewish children who were attempting to smuggle food into the Ghetto, Warsaw, 1939–43 (b/w photo), German Photographer (20th Century)/© SZ Photo/Bridgeman Images: 29; German Officers in Upper Castle, Vilna (photo)/Universal History Archive/UIG/Bridgeman Images: 36

LIBRARY OF CONGRESS CATALOGING-IN-PUBLICATION DATA

Blohm, Craig E., 1948-
 Holocaust resistance / by Craig E. Blohm.
  pages cm -- (Understanding the Holocaust series)
 Includes bibliographical references and index.
 ISBN-13: 978-1-60152-846-9 (hardback)
 ISBN-10: 1-60152-846-9 (hardback)
 1. World War, 1939-1945--Jewish resistance--Juvenile literature. 2. Holocaust, Jewish (1939-1945)--Juvenile literature. I. Title.
 D810.J4B525 2016
 940.53'1832--dc23
                                                                2015003530

CONTENTS

IMPORTANT EVENTS OF THE HOLOCAUST

1937
Buchenwald concentration camp is established in east-central Germany.

1941
Germany invades the Soviet Union; the Germans massacre about one hundred thousand Jews, Roma (Gypsies), Communists, and others at Babi Yar in Ukraine; the United States declares war on Japan and Germany after Japan attacks Pearl Harbor.

1920
The Nazi Party publishes its 25-point program declaring its intention to segregate Jews from so-called Aryan society and to eliminate the political, legal, and civil rights of Germany's Jewish population.

1925
Adolf Hitler's autobiographical manifesto *Mein Kampf* is published; in it he outlines his political ideology and future plans for Germany and calls for the violent elimination of the world's Jews.

1940
The Warsaw ghetto—a 1.3 square mile (3.4 sq km) area sealed off from the rest of the city by high walls, barbed wire, and armed guards—is established in Poland.

1920 / 1934 1936 1938 1940

1918
The Treaty of Versailles, marking the formal end of World War I and a humiliating defeat for Germany, is signed.

1935
The Nuremberg Laws, excluding German Jews from citizenship and depriving them of the right to vote and hold public office, are enacted.

1939
Germany invades Poland, igniting World War II in Europe; in Warsaw, Jews are forced to wear white armbands with a blue Star of David.

1933
Hitler is appointed Germany's chancellor; the Gestapo is formed; Dachau concentration camp is established.

1938
Violent anti-Jewish attacks known as *Kristallnacht* (Night of Broken Glass) take place throughout greater Germany; the first *Kindertransport* (children's transport) arrives in Great Britain with thousands of Jewish children seeking refuge from Nazi persecution.

1942
The Nazi plan to annihilate Europe's Jews (the Final Solution) is outlined at the Wannsee Conference in Berlin; deportations of about 1.5 million Jews to killing centers in Poland begin

1944
Allied forces carry out the D-Day invasion at Normandy in France; diplomats in Budapest offer protection to Jews.

1948
The State of Israel is established as a homeland for the world's Jews.

1946
The International Military Tribunal imposes death and prison sentences during the Nuremberg Trials.

1949
Argentina grants asylum to Josef Mengele, the notorious SS doctor who performed medical experiments on prisoners in Auschwitz.

1942   1944   1946   1948   1970

1943
Despite armed Jewish resistance, the Nazis move to liquidate ghettos in Poland and the Soviet Union; Denmark actively resists Nazi attempts to deport its Jewish citizens.

1960
In Argentina, Israeli intelligence agents abduct Adolf Eichmann, one of the masterminds of the Holocaust; he is brought to Israel to stand trial for crimes against the Jewish people.

1945
Allied forces liberate Auschwitz, Buchenwald, and Dachau concentration camps; Hitler commits suicide; World War II ends with the surrender of Germany and Japan; the Nuremberg Trials begin with war crimes indictments against leading Nazis.

1981
More than ten thousand survivors attend the first World Gathering of Jewish Holocaust Survivors in Israel; a similar gathering two years later in Washington, DC, attracts twenty thousand people.

1947
The UN General Assembly adopts a resolution partitioning Palestine into Jewish and Arab states; Holocaust survivor Simon Wiesenthal opens a center in Austria to search for Nazis who have evaded justice.

The Myth of Passivity

Primo Levi, a Jewish chemist who lived through the Holocaust, stood in front of a fifth-grade class describing what his life was like in the Auschwitz killing center during World War II. After telling his young audience about gas chambers, watch towers, and barbed wire fences, one of the students had a question for the elderly survivor: "But how come you didn't escape?"[1] The young boy could not know that his question was one that had become widespread in the years since the war had ended and the concentration camps closed. As people around the world gradually learned about the atrocities committed by the Nazis, many could not understand why the Jews passively submitted to such cruelty without at least attempting to fight back. The question that hounded Holocaust survivors for years usually took the form of "Why didn't they resist?" The simple fact, confirmed by countless survivor stories and the historical record, is that many Jews *did* resist.

Armed Resistance

Despite the horrific conditions that confronted the Jews in the ghettos and concentration camps that the Nazis established in conquered territories, brave prisoners defied their captors in numerous ways. Escape was one form of resistance, and many who managed to break away joined groups of armed rebels called partisans. Fighting from hidden forest enclaves, the partisans obstructed the Nazi war effort through sabotage, theft, and physical harassment. Other resisters attempted to overthrow the administration of the ghettos and camps. In Warsaw, the capital of Poland, Jews staged the largest ghetto uprising of the Holocaust. Rebellions were also instigated in the Bialystok, Vilna, and Czestochowa ghettos. In the Nazi killing centers of Auschwitz, Sobibor, and Treblinka, inmates secretly organized rebellions, carrying out their plans by attacking camp guards with stolen guns, explosives, and anything they could find to turn into makeshift weapons. During these uprisings Jewish rebels killed guards, destroyed gas chambers and other camp buildings, and enabled inmates to escape.

Most acts of armed resistance were doomed to failure. Not only did the rebels ultimately pay with their lives, but the entire Jewish population was at risk. Jewish archivist and social activist Emanuel Ringelblum notes that "if even one German is killed, its outcome may lead to a slaughter of a whole community, or even of many communities."[2]

Spiritual Resistance

Not everyone had the will or the opportunity to openly resist the Nazis. But there were other, nonviolent ways of rebelling against the inhuman conditions in the ghettos and camps. Faced with the possibility of being annihilated as a religion, a people, and a culture, Jews sought to preserve their identity with nonviolent acts of spiritual resistance. Not only did such acts attempt to undermine their Nazi captors, they provided the prisoners with an inner strength that they believed was essential to their survival. "Every Jew who remains alive," wrote Rabbi Avraham Shalom Goldberg in the Warsaw ghetto in 1942, "sanctifies the Name of God among many. He is indeed a man of courage because he will not submit to the Nazis and will not extinguish his precious life."[3]

Spiritual resistance took many forms. In the ghettos the forbidden act of educating children was accomplished surreptitiously by teachers who received small portions of food as payment. Concerts, plays, and lectures helped to lift the spirits of the Jews in the larger ghettos. Spiritual resistance was a dangerous endeavor in the brutal environment of the concentration camps. Nevertheless, many imprisoned Jews were able to secretly perform cultural and religious activities such as writing, painting, singing songs, and celebrating Hanukkah, the Jewish festival of lights, with makeshift candles. Jews working in forced labor camps and German factories seized opportunities to sabotage their work, resulting in defective equipment being supplied to German troops on the front lines.

For many Jewish prisoners simply living another day and hoping for a better future was an act of spiritual resistance. But for some, when life in the camps became unbearable, dying with dignity was

Nazis arrest Jews in Poland's Warsaw ghetto after the 1943 ghetto uprising. Jews engaged in resistance efforts in ghettos and in concentration camps, and by joining with armed units of partisans who roamed the European countryside.

the only remaining choice. Suicide was, perhaps, the ultimate act of resistance, snatching the decision of life or death from the hands of the Nazi executioners.

Helping the Resistance

While Jews were resisting the Nazis from inside the ghettos and camps, many non-Jews risked their lives to help them in their struggle. In the early stages of the Holocaust thousands of Jews were hurried to safety by compassionate people who provided them with transportation and false identity papers. For those who could not escape, others jeopardized their own safety to provide hiding places throughout occupied Europe, sometimes keeping Jews safe from Nazi search parties for years. Children, especially vulnerable to the evils of the Holocaust, were shown particular kindness by those in the non-Jewish community. Just before the outbreak of World War II a rescue mission called

Kindertransport brought some ten thousand children to safety in Great Britain. The tiny French village of Le Chambon-sur-Lignon became a refuge for about five thousand Jews, mostly children, who were persecuted by France's Nazi-controlled Vichy government.

Exposing the Myth

Despite all the evidence supporting Jewish resistance, many people, including some historians, supported the idea that the Jews went to the gas chambers "like sheep to the slaughter." In 1961 Holocaust scholar Raul Hilberg argued that historically the Jews had "unlearned the art of resistance. . . . The Jews could not resist."[4] Bruno Bettelheim, a psychologist and Holocaust survivor, wrote in 1960 that the Jews "like lemmings, marched themselves to their own death."[5] Most historians have since refuted the myth of Jews passively submitting to their captors as more and more stories of heroic resistance have emerged. "Under conditions of human degradation and suffering," writes historian Nechama Tec, "Jews were determined to survive—they refused to become passive victims."[6]

"Under conditions of human degradation and suffering, Jews were determined to survive—they refused to become passive victims."[6]

—Historian Nechama Tec.

The horrors that the Jews experienced during the Holocaust are unimaginable to most people today. But just as the Holocaust must never be forgotten, so too should the memory of the courageous individuals who risked everything to resist the Nazi system be kept alive.

CHAPTER ONE

Fighting Back

For Estusia Wajcblum, the end of the workday at the Weichsel-Union-Metallwerke factory, a munitions plant in the Auschwitz death camp, meant a welcome respite from a grueling twelve-hour shift. Twenty-year-old Wajcblum worked in the factory's *Pulverraum* (powder room), inserting explosive black powder into detonators destined for German bombs. As she rose from her workbench, she picked up a small rag and quietly placed it in a false-bottomed tin. In the rag was a small amount of black powder she had secretly taken from her bench. Seven other women in the *Pulverraum* were also stealing the valuable explosive. The black powder was smuggled out of the factory and used to make grenades and bombs for a planned rebellion in the camp.

The smuggling of explosives and other weapons was part of an extensive pattern of clandestine Jewish rebellion against the Nazi regime. Resistance organizations were established in many of the ghettos and camps to secretly plan attacks against the Nazis. Although the odds against the Jews were overwhelming, their numerous acts of armed resistance demonstrate their extreme courage while suffering under extreme oppression.

The Warsaw Ghetto

In October 1940 German authorities in the Polish capital of Warsaw began rounding up Jews and moving them into an area of the city that normally held about one hundred thousand residents. By November 16 nearly four hundred thousand Polish Jews were living in the Warsaw ghetto under appalling conditions. Typhus, a deadly disease transmitted by lice, was rampant, and bodies of people who had died of disease or starvation became a common sight on the streets.

Almost from the beginning, secret underground groups were organized to defy the ghetto's administration and provide aid and comfort to the beleaguered residents. Most of these groups were made up of idealistic young Jews such as twenty-three-year-old Mordecai Anielewicz. Born in Warsaw, Anielewicz taught children and published an underground newspaper in the ghetto. When news of Nazi mass murders of Jews in the occupied eastern territories reached him, Anielewicz knew that a plan for a more active resistance was needed.

Starving children await help or death—whichever comes first—in the Warsaw ghetto in 1941. Jews forced to live within the confines of the ghetto endured appalling conditions.

Founding ZOB

On July 22, 1942, an order of relocation of the residents of the Warsaw ghetto was given to the ghetto's *Judenrat*, or governing council. It stated that "all Jewish persons living in Warsaw, regardless of age and sex, will be resettled in the East."[7] Most ghetto residents believed that they were being sent to work camps, but some suspected the Nazis had a more sinister destination. One Warsaw underground newspaper stated, "We know that Hitler's system of murder, slaughter and robbery leads steadily to a dead end and the destruction of the Jews."[8] The Nazis immediately began rounding up Jews and deporting them to the Treblinka killing center. By mid-September only about sixty thousand people were left in the ghetto.

Anielewicz was away from the ghetto when he learned about the deportation. Hurrying back to Warsaw, he formed an armed resistance group by consolidating many of the existing underground factions. The Jewish Fighting Organization (known by its Polish acronym ZOB) was established on July 28, 1942, with Anielewicz as commander. ZOB's first test came on January 18, 1943, when Nazis once more began deporting Jews from the ghetto. Nine ZOB fighters, led by Anielewicz, attacked the Nazi escorts. In the street battle that followed, many of the ZOB fighters were killed. After four days of fighting, the Nazis withdrew from the ghetto. ZOB's militant response to the January deportations was the first occurrence of armed resistance against the Nazis. It would not be the last.

The Uprising Begins

Since their January battle members of ZOB had been acquiring weapons, making grenades, and training for the next round of deportations. A network of underground bunkers and apartment refuges was created for civilians to hide from the Nazis and for ZOB fighters to use as home bases. On April 19, 1943, the eve of the Jewish Passover celebration, the Nazis stormed the Warsaw ghetto for the final deportation operation. Two thousand troops invaded the ghetto, supported by a tank, two armored vehicles, and several howitzers and anti-aircraft guns. Against

Farewell from the Ghetto

As the Nazis closed in on the remaining resistance fighters hidden in the Warsaw ghetto, underground commander Mordecai Anielewicz wrote a final heartfelt letter to his comrade outside the ghetto, Yitzhak Zuckerman.

It is impossible to put into words what we have been through. One thing is clear, what happened exceeded our boldest dreams. The Germans ran twice from the ghetto. One of our companies held out for 40 minutes and another for more than 6 hours. The mine set in the "brushmakers" area exploded. Several of our companies attacked the dispersing Germans. . . .

It is impossible to describe the conditions under which the Jews of the ghetto are now living. Only a few will be able to hold out. The remainder will die sooner or later. Their fate is decided. In almost all the hiding places in which thousands are concealing themselves it is not possible to light a candle for lack of air. . . .

Peace go with you, my friend! Perhaps we may still meet again! The dream of my life has risen to become fact. Self-defense in the ghetto will have been a reality. Jewish armed resistance and revenge are facts. I have been witness to the magnificent, heroic fighting of Jewish men in battle.

M. Anielewicz
Ghetto, April 23, 1943

Shoah Resource Center, "Last Letter from Ghetto Revolt Commander Mordecai Anielewicz, Warsaw." www.yadvashem.org.

this assault the Jewish force numbered about six hundred fighters. Although outnumbered, the ZOB fighters had advance warning of the German assault and, along with another resistance group (the Jewish Military Union, or ZZW), were lying in wait. *Generalleutnant* Jürgen

Stroop of the SS (*Schutzstaffel*, or "protection squadron") commanded the operation. In his official report of the first day of action he wrote,

> Hardly had the units fallen in, strong concerted fire-concentration by the Jews and bandits [Polish underground fighters]. The tank used in this action and the two heavy armored cars pelted with Molotov cocktails (incendiary bottles). Tank twice set on fire. Owing to this enemy counterattack, we had at first to take the units back. Losses in the first attack: 12 men.[9]

The Nazis rounded up 580 Jewish civilians for deportation on the first day. The Jewish fighters were able to escape, while the Nazis regrouped for another attack. Several days of intense street fighting followed, with the ZOB and ZZW forces staging quick strikes against the Nazis and then retreating to the safety of their bunkers. These tactics forced the Germans to change their plan of attack: Instead of fighting the Jews in the streets, they began burning the entire ghetto to the ground, building by building.

Trial by Fire

By setting fires in the ghetto the Nazis were able to drive the Jews from their hiding places and march them to Warsaw's *Umschlagplatz* (central square) for deportation. On April 23 Stroop reported that "the action will be completed on this very day."[10] His optimism was premature, as the Jewish fighters continued their attacks. "The fighting is fierce," reported a ZOB communiqué. "The Jewish resistance fighters are hurting the enemy. They are setting fires to the factories and warehouses of the German war industry."[11] But the tide of battle was turning. Plagued by lack of ammunition and heavy losses, the ZOB and ZZW fighters were forced to retreat to the bunkers. Anielewicz, along with eighty fighters and three hundred civilians, dug in at the ZOB headquarters bunker at 18 Mila Street.

"The fighting is fierce. The Jewish resistance fighters are hurting the enemy. They are setting fires to the factories and warehouses of the German war industry."[11]

—ZOB communiqué.

Visitors at an Israeli museum view a replica of the 18 Mila Street bunker used as the headquarters of ZOB, one of the Jewish resistance groups in the Warsaw ghetto. ZOB fighters died in the bunker after putting up one last effort at resistance.

By early May the Warsaw ghetto was engulfed in flames. Jewish civilians flushed out of hiding were shot or herded to the *Umschlag-platz*. On May 8 German forces surrounded ZOB headquarters. The civilians surrendered, and the ZOB fighters put up one last effort at resistance. After a two-hour battle, some fighters committed suicide, while German poison gas killed the others; Anielewicz died with his comrades. By May 16, with the Warsaw ghetto a smoldering ruin, Stroop's final report to his superiors stated, "The former Jewish residential district [a German euphemism for the ghetto] in Warsaw no longer exists."[12] Although Stroop reported only about one hundred German casualties, other less-biased sources place the number at three hundred or more. Despite the defeat of the Jewish resisters, a small remnant managed to escape to fight another day.

The Warsaw ghetto uprising was the first and largest armed Jewish revolt against the Nazis. Its importance is confirmed by Polish military historian Jerzy Kirchmayer, who writes, "The Warsaw Ghetto fell after a heroic fight, but the idea of armed struggle, in the name of which the insurgents had died, reached beyond the walls, survived and endured until victory."[13]

Rebellion at Bialystok

Against the vast superiority of Nazi forces, the Warsaw ghetto uprising was doomed to failure. But even without a victory in battle, the courageous ZOB fighters provided an example for the Jews of occupied Poland. One Jewish activist who helped spread the idea of resistance against the Nazis to other ghettos was Mordechai Tenenbaum.

With forged papers identifying him as "Jozef Tamaroff," Tenenbaum was able to travel throughout occupied Poland, gathering information about Nazi activities and organizing resistance movements in the ghettos. In July 1942 twenty-six-year-old Tenenbaum was in the Warsaw ghetto, where he assisted in the creation of ZOB after the first wave of mass deportations. By November he had arrived at the ghetto in Bialystok, a small town in northeastern Poland. There he found the town surrounded by Nazis and fifty thousand Jews confined behind wood and barbed wire fences. Tenenbaum went to work helping to create a united resistance front out of several underground groups. The combined forces eventually numbered about five hundred fighters.

Since its inception the Bialystok ghetto had become an industrial center in occupied Poland. Most ghetto residents were forced to work in factories, mills, and workshops, making supplies for the *Wehrmacht* (German armed forces). For a while this vital labor kept the Bialystok Jews safe from extermination. But in February 1943 the Nazis swooped into the ghetto and shot to death about one thousand Jews in the streets. After this bloodbath they rounded up ten thousand Jews and sent them to the Treblinka killing center. As the deportation *aktion* (operation) progressed, the underground hesitated, undecided about whether they should fight back. Later, Tenenbaum regretted the decision to hold back. "We did not react," he wrote in a letter to his sister. "All we managed to do was save our comrades. For had we thrown our grenades, no one would have been alive to tell the story. Our chance will yet come. We shall yet throw them."[14] The time to throw the grenades came six months later.

The August Revolt

At about 2:00 a.m. on August 16, 1943, the final *aktion* to liquidate the ghetto began. Three rings of heavily armed soldiers supported by armored vehicles encircled the ghetto quietly so as not to raise alarm. When underground members realized what was happening, they quickly distributed weapons and prepared to launch the resistance. As the Germans began marching Jews to a central point for deportation, Tenenbaum's fighters urged the crowd to disobey orders and join the resistance. A proclamation posted on ghetto walls exhorted, "Do not go freely to your death! Fight for your life until your last breath!"[15] The resisters set fires at points in the ghetto fence to create openings for the Jews to escape, but the people were too terrified to attempt a breakout.

> "Do not go freely to your death! Fight for your life until your last breath!"[15]
>
> —Proclamation in the Bialystok ghetto.

At just before 9:30 a.m. the armed resistance began, engaging the Germans in the narrow streets and setting the ghetto's factories ablaze. Haika Grosman, a female member of the underground, describes one battle:

> Suddenly we were under fire. One man lay in his blood. The house went up in flames; the adjoining houses were also burning like matchboxes. The house was no longer a shelter, we had to retreat. . . . Now they were shooting from the embankment. They, too, had retreated firing with heavy weapons. A machine gun began its rat-a-tat of death. . . . We repeatedly attacked and retreated.[16]

The Bialystok uprising lasted five days, with the German forces ultimately overpowering the rebels, who had exhausted their ammunition. The last holdouts, including Tenenbaum, were entrenched in a bunker that was finally overrun by the Germans on August 20. All the resisters died either from German fire or by committing suicide. The resistance fought bravely against great odds but could not save the more than thirty-five thousand Bialystok Jews from being transported to their deaths in the Holocaust camps.

The Treblinka Revolt

When the Nazis began liquidating the ghettos in 1942, hundreds of thousands of Jews and other people regarded as inferior were sent to labor camps and killing centers throughout Nazi-occupied Europe. Although the conditions at the camps were even more horrific than those in the ghettos, the commitment to resistance among many of the Jews remained strong. At several Nazi killing centers inmates staged armed revolts, fighting their captors against tremendous odds.

> "We all ran out of our barracks and took the stations that had been assigned to us. Within a matter of minutes, fires were raging all around."[17]
>
> —Treblinka uprising survivor Yankel Wiernik.

The German invasions of Czechoslovakia and Poland in 1939 and the conquering of France in 1940 demonstrated the seeming invincibility of Hitler's *Wehrmacht*. But the German defeat in the battle of Stalingrad, Russia, in February 1943, was the turning point of World War II in Europe. The Germans were in retreat, and the world realized that the defeat of Hitler's Third Reich was inevitable.

The news from Stalingrad and reports of the Warsaw ghetto rebellion encouraged the members of an underground resistance committee in the Treblinka killing center. They began to assemble an arsenal for a rebellion in which they planned to destroy the camp and enable the prisoners to escape. Along with procuring pistols and rifles, they created an unlikely "weapon" out of a portable chemical sprayer. Normally used to disinfect camp buildings, the rebels filled the device with gasoline to douse the structures and burn them down.

Marceli Galewski, the underground commander, set the date for the uprising for August 2, 1943. At a prearranged signal the rebels, armed with stolen pistols and rifles, attacked the camp's guards. "As soon as the signal shot rang out," recalls Treblinka survivor Yankel Wiernik, "the guard at the well had been killed and his weapons taken from him. We all ran out of our barracks and took the stations that had been assigned to us." The camp buildings, now soaked with gasoline, were ignited by homemade grenades and incendiary bottles. "Within a matter of minutes," continues Wiernik, "fires were raging all around."[17]

Although the guards were initially taken by surprise, they quickly regrouped and fought back against the insurgents. Concentrated machine-gun fire from the watchtowers mowed down many of the rebels. During the uprising some three hundred prisoners were able to escape. In the manhunt that followed, about two-thirds of the escapees were recaptured and ultimately murdered. Although Galewski managed to escape the camp, he was unable to outrun the Nazis and committed suicide rather than be taken captive.

Rebellion at Auschwitz

Fourteen months after the Treblinka revolt, Auschwitz, the largest of the Nazi killing centers, was the scene of another bloody rebellion. Every day, trains arrived at Auschwitz carrying Jews designated for extermination. Five crematoria (numbered I through V) operated twenty-four hours a day, burning the bodies of the people killed in the center's gas chambers. Jewish workers called *Sonderkommandos* were

Jewish prisoners known as Sonderkommandos use tongs to lift a dead body into an oven for cremation at Dachau concentration camp. In October 1945 a group of Auschwitz Sonderkommandos mounted a rebellion that ended with the execution of hundreds of Jews.

The Importance of the *Sonderkommando* Rebellion

Jewish historian Israel Gutman took part in the Warsaw ghetto uprising and witnessed the horrors of the Majdanek, Mauthausen, and Auschwitz camps. In Gutman's assessment of the 1944 *Sonderkommando* rebellion at Auschwitz, he considered the failed uprising a confirmation of the Jewish fighting spirit.

> And yet, despite the terrible Jewish losses . . . the day of the uprising of the Sonderkommando became a symbol of revenge and was an inspiration to the prisoners. In the place that had served for years as a field of slaughter for millions of victims, there fell the first Nazis in Auschwitz. And it was Jews who had done the fighting. In this gigantic camp where tens of thousands of prisoners were confined, a handful of Jews broke free of the pervasive spirit of submission and passive resignation to their cruel fate. The uprising of the Sonderkommando proved to the prisoners of diverse European nationalities that Jews knew how to fight for their lives.

Quoted in Nechama Tec, *Resistance: Jews and Christians Who Defied the Nazi Terror.* Oxford: Oxford University Press, 2013, p. 144.

forced to perform the gruesome task of transporting corpses from the gas chambers to the crematoria. The *Sonderkommandos* were kept alive as long as there were bodies to burn. But when the number of trains arriving at Auschwitz began to decline in 1944, they knew the Nazis could eliminate them at any time.

An underground resistance group in the camp had been planning an uprising for several months. Explosive black powder, smuggled to the resistance by women working in the Weichsel-Union-Metallwerke munitions plant at Auschwitz, was used to make grenades for the uprising. When word came on October 7, 1944, that the end was near, the *Sonderkommandos* went into action at crematorium IV. Historian Igor Bartosik describes the rebellion.

> During the unequal fight, the prisoners were able to set fire to the crematorium. Soon after that, the action was supported by their fellow prisoners from the crematorium II. They cut wires of the fence and started to run away towards the South. . . . The refugees were however killed by the SS pursuit units. As a result of the revolt and executions made by the SS-men, approximately 400 out of 600 prisoners were killed. The prisoners managed to kill three of them and hurt more than ten of armed SS men.[18]

The women who had smuggled the explosives to the resistance were tortured and hanged for their part in the rebellion. The damage to crematorium IV inflicted by the rebels put it out of commission. Soon all killings at Auschwitz were halted and the remaining crematoria dismantled. On January 25, 1945, the camp was liberated by troops of the Soviet Red Army, who discovered about seventy-five hundred prisoners still alive.

The Courage of the Resisters

The Jews who instigated armed resistance in the ghettos and camps knew that they were fighting against a superior force and that they had almost no chance of success. Yet they never hesitated to risk their lives to damage the Nazi camps or allow a few Jews to escape. Their courage provided an inspiration to other Jews to fight back against their Nazi oppressors. It even impressed Nazi propaganda minister Joseph Goebbels, who wrote in his diary that the resistance "shows what the Jews are capable of when they have arms in their hands."[19]

CHAPTER TWO

Spiritual Resistance

One of the most famous books written during the Holocaust is a small red-and-white-checked diary belonging to a young girl named Anne Frank. Within its covers the diary holds the thoughts of the Jewish teenager who, with her family, spent more than two years hiding from the Nazis in a commercial building in Amsterdam in the Netherlands.

Writing in her diary allowed Frank to maintain her dignity, her humanity, her spirit in the midst of so much extreme degradation and inhumanity. The diary provided a young girl with a personal, nonviolent way of fighting back against the horrors perpetrated by the Nazis—it offered a type of spiritual resistance. Other people practiced spiritual resistance in their own ways—sometimes through diaries or letters but also through art, music, religion, and literature. Not everyone had this ability or opportunity. But those who did, like Anne Frank, defeated the Nazis by not giving in to their brutality, even in the face of death.

Pictures of Life in the Ghettos

Mendel Grossman was an artist with a camera. Born in Poland in 1913, he demonstrated a gift for drawing and painting at a young age. Grossman went on to apply his natural talent to photography, eventually becoming a professional photographer. His keen eye and innovative images of a traveling theater troupe brought him fame as a photographer of the performing arts. But his most important photographs were those he took in a Polish ghetto.

In early 1940 Grossman was one of more than two hundred thousand Jews forced into the newly established ghetto in the Polish city of Lodz. His photographic skills landed him a job in the ghetto's official photography section, where he took pictures for use on identity cards and photographed official ceremonies. This work allowed him access to the equipment he needed for a more important, but highly illegal, job. Walking around the ghetto wearing a loose-fitting coat under which he hid his camera, Grossman documented life in the ghetto on film. His images of Jews rounded up for deportation, children pulling heavily laden carts like beasts of burden, and the corpses of those murdered by the Nazis, tell of the tragedy of the ghetto. Despite suffering from a heart condition, Grossman often climbed to the top of buildings to get a unique perspective on his subjects below.

Over the course of four years in the Lodz ghetto, Grossman shot more than ten thousand photographs. When liquidation of the ghetto was imminent in August 1944, he hid the photographic negatives in the walls and cellar of his ghetto apartment. Deported to a concentration camp in Germany, Grossman died on a death march from

Women work with strips of leather in Poland's Lodz ghetto in 1941. Other scenes of ghetto life were captured in the photographs of Mendel Grossman, a Jewish photographer who was later deported to a concentration camp.

The White Rose

As a teenager Hans Scholl joined the Hitler Youth movement but eventually became disillusioned with the group's anti-Semitism and blind allegiance to Adolf Hitler. After World War II began, Hans and his sister, Sophie, were enrolled at the University of Munich. They shared their opposition to Hitler's regime with fellow students and their philosophy professor, Kurt Huber. They named their group the White Rose, and its informal discussions soon turned to nonviolent action.

In 1942 a leaflet entitled "The White Rose" began appearing in the mailboxes of a random selection of Munich citizens. Published anonymously, the leaflet encouraged its readers to "offer passive resistance—resistance, wherever you may be, prevent the continuation of this atheistic war machine before it is too late." It ended with the plea, "We ask that you copy this document . . . and pass it on!"

Five more leaflets followed, each one calling on German citizens to oppose the Nazi regime. The White Rose printed and distributed more than ten thousand leaflets by mail or by simply leaving them in public places. Allied bombers even dropped copies of the sixth leaflet over Germany. On February 18, 1943, while distributing leaflets at the university, Hans and Sophie were spotted by a Nazi Party member and subsequently arrested by the Gestapo. Four days later they were tried and executed; Huber was put to death five months later. Despite its short existence, the White Rose group proved that not all Germans followed the Nazi Party line.

Center for White Rose Studies, Leaflet 1. www.white-rose-studies.org.

the camp, still clutching his camera. His negatives were eventually recovered and brought by family to Israel. Although many were lost in Israel's War for Independence in 1948, the surviving images are testimony to a man who risked his life and defied the authorities to preserve a record of ghetto life for future generations.

The Power of Words

Photographs from the Holocaust present images of human suffering in stark black and white; some are almost too disturbing to look at. The written word was also a powerful tool used by Jews in the ghettos and camps to record their daily experiences as well as express their innermost thoughts and feelings. Many diaries, letters, and stories were buried or otherwise hidden from the Nazis with the hope that they would be discovered after the war.

Working in the crematoria of the Nazi killing centers, the *Sonderkommandos* were eyewitnesses to the worst horrors of the Holocaust. Realizing that their knowledge of the killing process would ultimately mean their own death, many wrote accounts of their gruesome work on any scrap of paper they could find. Zalman Gradowski, a *Sonderkommando* at Auschwitz, buried his eighty-one-page diary in a jar a month before the ill-fated uprising at the killing center. Other *Sonderkommandos* hid their own personal documents as well. To the eventual discoverer of his diary, Gradowski wrote,

> Dear finder, search everywhere, in every inch of soil. Tens of documents are buried under it, mine and those of other persons, which will throw light on everything that was happening here. . . . We ourselves have lost hope of being able to live to see the moment of liberation. . . . May the future judge us on the basis of my notes and may the world see in them, if only one drop, the minimum, of this tragic world amidst which we had lived.[20]

In his diary Gradowski describes the Nazi process of murdering Jews, from their arrival at the train platform to their deaths in the gas chambers and disposal in the crematorium where he worked. He also wrote a brief but poignant description of his time at Auschwitz: "The dark night is my friend, tears and screams are my songs, the fire of sacrifice is my light, the atmosphere of death is my perfume. Hell is my home."[21] Gradowski was hanged for his part in the

> "The dark night is my friend, tears and screams are my songs, the fire of sacrifice is my light, the atmosphere of death is my perfume. Hell is my home."[21]
>
> —Auschwitz *Sonderkommando* Zalman Gradowski.

failed *Sonderkommando* rebellion. But after the discovery of his diary when Auschwitz was liberated in 1945, Gradowski's words live on.

Oneg Shabbat

Much of the literature of the Holocaust would have been lost forever if not for the foresight of a social activist named Emanuel Ringelblum. When the Warsaw ghetto was established in 1940 Ringelblum was one of the nearly four hundred thousand Jews locked behind the brick walls and barbed wire. As a historian, he saw the need to document the growing persecution of the Jews. But Ringelblum knew he could not undertake such a massive task alone.

Along with writing his own diary of the Warsaw ghetto, Ringelblum began assembling a small group to collect documents describing ghetto life and the torment endured by the Jews. Meeting on Saturdays, the Jewish Sabbath, the group adopted the code name *Oneg Shabbat* ("Joy of the Sabbath"). For nearly three years, from 1939 to 1942, the underground group created an archive by collecting letters, diaries, photographs, posters, and numerous other documents about the ghetto. Group members interviewed new arrivals to the ghetto, amassing pages of information about other ghettos and Nazi camps. The *Oneg Shabbat* archives contain numerous personal observations, such as the following diary entry written by Abraham Lewin, a teacher in the ghetto:

> "The Germans' lust for Jewish blood knows no bounds. It is a bottomless pit. Future generations will not believe it. But this is the unembellished truth, plain and simple."[22]
>
> —Abraham Lewin, teacher in the Warsaw ghetto.

Sunday, 16 August, 1942

The Germans' lust for Jewish blood knows no bounds. It is a bottomless pit. Future generations will not believe it. But this is the unembellished truth, plain and simple. A bitter, horrifying truth. The Jewish police have received an order that each one of them must bring five people to be transported [to the death camps]. Since there are 2000 police, they will have to find 10,000 victims. If they do not fulfil their quotas they are liable to the death-penalty.[22]

26

As the final destruction of the Warsaw ghetto drew near, the members of *Oneg Shabbat* hid the archives in metal boxes and milk cans and buried them in three locations under the rubble of the ghetto. The first two caches were discovered in 1946 and 1950, giving the world a glimpse of life in the ghetto. The third location has yet to be found.

Keeping the Faith

Documenting the horrors of the Holocaust for future generations through words and images was an important aspect of spiritual resistance. Equally vital for survival under such terrible conditions was the maintaining of Jewish faith and identity.

Religious devotion has been central to Jewish history and culture for thousands of years. The freedom to practice one's faith was stripped from the Jews when they were deported to the ghettos. In many ghettos Jews were forced to work on Saturdays (the Jewish Sabbath) and on High Holy Days, traditionally days of rest and prayer. Some rabbis counseled their congregants to avoid such work if possible. "In the Kovno ghetto," writes Holocaust historian Lucy Dawidowicz, "pious Jews sought assignment to labor brigades that did not work on the Sabbath, even though that entailed forfeiting extra food rations or a chance for less strenuous or unpleasant work."[23]

Clandestine religious celebrations were held despite the repressive atmosphere of the concentration camps. "Every Friday night, the Sabbath," recalls Alice Lok, who was fifteen years old when she was sent to Auschwitz, "we'd pray where we could assemble secretly—the latrine. Other children joined us for these prayers."[24] At the camp Jewish women made Sabbath candles from hollowed-out potatoes or bits of margarine. Kiddush cups, goblets or other drinking vessels used in the Sabbath ceremony, were found in the ruins of the Belzec killing center after the war. These artifacts confirm that the Sabbath was being observed there despite the penalty of discovery, which was death. Jews in Bergen-Belsen observed Yom Kippur, the holiest day of the Jewish year. Hanukkah was celebrated at Auschwitz, as related by survivor Israel Cohen.

> I thought about my family at Hanukkah, about our father's joy and fervor when he lit the menorah [nine-branched candelabrum]. And then I knew we had to find a way to at least

light Hanukkah candles and say the prayers. And we did. My spoon served as the menorah. Someone gave margarine he had saved to be the oil. We unraveled threads from our uniforms and wove them into wicks and then lit the wicks.[25]

For some, the brutality of life in the concentration camps destroyed even the strongest faith. But for others, their faith sustained them. David Halivni, a teenager in the Gross-Rosen labor camp writes, "I had philosophical questions and doubts: Since there were so many cruelties, God cannot exist. He would not have permitted it. But without God it is even more cruel. He gave man the power, and God gave man his free will."[26]

Smuggling in the Ghettos

When the Germans created the ghettos and camps, those confined within were effectively sealed off from the rest of the world and forced to survive on whatever food their captors provided. Those rations were meager. In the Warsaw ghetto Jews were allowed 181 calories per day, about 10 percent of a German soldier's daily ration. According to Raul Hilberg, the monthly allotment of food per person in the Lodz ghetto was "less than one and one-half pounds of meat, one egg, 12 pounds of potatoes, and two ounces of cheese."[27] Starvation was rampant, and as many as six thousand people died each month of malnutrition and resultant disease, their bodies left in the streets. To combat starvation Jews began smuggling food from outside the ghettos. Children were often called upon to be the smugglers, as their size and agility were decided advantages for the hazardous job. Most of these young smugglers were from ten to fourteen years old. They slipped through barbed wire or under fences, sometimes traveling through sewers to reach their destinations beyond the walls of the ghetto. Along with food, the children also brought in much-needed

> "I had philosophical questions and doubts: Since there were so many cruelties, God cannot exist. He would not have permitted it. But without God it is even more cruel. He gave man the power, and God gave man his free will."[26]
>
> —Gross-Rosen survivor David Halivni.

Young Jews caught smuggling food into the Warsaw ghetto are arrested by German police. Because of their size and agility, children were often given the job of smuggling food to help feed starving ghetto residents.

medicine and clothing. The children risked the same punishment as adults if they were caught: a beating or a bullet from a Nazi pistol.

Women also took part in acts of smuggling. One group of female *kashariyot* (couriers) operated in German-occupied territory outside the ghettos, using falsified documents to hide their true identities. The courage of the *kashariyot* was noted by Ringelblum in his diary in 1942: "They are in mortal danger every day. . . . Without a murmur, without a moment of hesitation, they accept and carry out the most dangerous missions. . . . Nothing stands in their way. Nothing deters them."[28]

The *kashariyot* smuggled medicine, food, weapons and ammunition, and money into the ghettos. One of the most important commodities they carried was information. The women became a link (the word *kashariyot* comes from the Hebrew word for "connection")

Yitzkhak Viner: Poet of the Ghetto

Poetry was one way for many Jews trapped in the ghettos to express their hopes, fears, and dreams. Yitzkhak Viner, a resident of the Lodz ghetto, wrote the following poem entitled "Good It Is to Have Two Eyes." It was originally written in Yiddish and is preserved in the archives of *Oneg Shabbat*, a group formed by ghetto residents to document their lives during the Holocaust.

Good it is to have two eyes
Anything I want they see:
Boats and trains, horses, cars,
everything there is on earth.
But it happens sometimes that
I want to see a person laugh . . .
But instead I see a corpse,
stretched out in the street.
When I want to see one laugh—
his eyes are closed forever.

Good it is to have two ears,
Anything I want they hear:
Songs, plays, concert of words,
Street cars, bells, anything.
I want to hear the children voices sing,
but ears hear only screams . . .
of two children near a corpse.
When I want youthful song—
Crying children hours long.

Good it is to have two hands,
every year to till the land,
banging iron day and night,
makes the wheels to till . . .
Wheels are standing silent, still,
People's hands are obsolete,
Cold and darkness in the house . . .
Hands digging a grave . . .
Good it is to have two hands—
I write poems about the truth—

Yitzkhak Viner, "Gut iz hobn oign tvey," translated by Sarah Traister Moskovitz as "Good It Is to Have Two Eyes." Poetry in Hell. www.poetryinhell.org.

to the events in the world outside the ghetto walls. They brought underground newspapers, letters, and information from radio newscasts to the Jews in the ghettos, informing them of, among other things, the true destinations of the deportation trains that went not to labor camps, as the Nazis claimed, but to the gas chambers of the death camps. Equally important as the contraband the *kashariyot* carried was the image they presented. To the oppressed Jews, these brave women who risked everything to provide help to the helpless were true heroines, real-life examples of the spirit of the resistance.

Resistance Through the Arts

Smuggling food helped fill the physical needs of the ghetto residents. But just as important in such a repressive environment was the desire to express their emotional needs. One way that people express their emotions is through artistic endeavors such as painting, poetry, drama, and literature. For those persecuted by the Nazis during the Holocaust, such expression was often the only way of coping with their situation. Much of the art of the Holocaust had to be done in secret for fear of retribution. Although the Nazis starved the Jews and forbade any religious and educational activities, in some ghettos they allowed Jews to participate in the arts.

In 1941 Theresienstadt, a fortified town in northwest Czechoslovakia, was converted to a ghetto (it also served as a transit camp) where some 140,000 Jews were interned between 1941 and 1945. Like all the Holocaust ghettos, conditions there were appalling, with overcrowding, malnutrition, and disease taking their toll on the population. What made Theresienstadt unique was its large community of artists, writers, and performers, both amateur and professional, who were allowed the freedom to practice their arts. This provided a rich cultural environment unknown in other ghettos. Many of the artists interned at Theresienstadt produced official works of art for the ghetto administration, while creating their personal artistic expressions in their off hours.

Cultural activities at Theresienstadt included dramas staged by professional actors, lectures presented by scholars, and musical performances. According to historian David Altschuler, "Actors, musicians, comics, singers, and dancers all entertained small groups who came together for a few hours to forget their daily terror and despair."[29] A youth opera entitled *Brundibár* was smuggled into Theresienstadt and performed more than fifty times by the ghetto's children. An adult opera, *Der Kaiser von Atlantis* (The Emperor of Atlantis) was written by two inmates in 1943. The Nazis did not allow the opera to be performed because they saw the Kaiser character as a sly satire of Adolf Hitler. Helga Weissová-Hošková, who arrived at Theresienstadt in 1941, recalls music in the ghetto. "Many of us came from musical families, and there were very great musicians among us. Each person was allowed 50 kilos of luggage and smuggled in musical instruments, even though it had been forbidden for Jews to own them. So no wonder the beauty of music and art bloomed in that real-life hell."[30]

The visual arts, including painting, drawing, and sculpture, also found expression in the death camps. Halina Olomucki began draw-

A drawing made in secret by an Auschwitz prisoner is displayed in a 2011 "Forbidden Art" exhibit in Poland. Some prisoners used art to express themselves and to document the horrors taking place around them.

ing in the Warsaw ghetto and continued when she was sent to several camps, finally ending up at Auschwitz. There she painted signs for the Nazis, for which she received additional rations of bread and cheese. But Olomucki secretly drew scenes depicting camp life as well. "I made drawings in the camps, using whatever scanty materials I could gather together."[31] Many of her fellow inmates at Auschwitz asked her to draw portraits of themselves or their loved ones, to provide a lasting memorial to those who might be sent to the gas chambers at any moment. Her stark

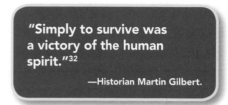

"Simply to survive was a victory of the human spirit."[32]

—Historian Martin Gilbert.

pencil sketches reflect the fear, despair, and sadness in the faces of the women of Auschwitz. Much of Olomucki's work survived the Holocaust and is preserved in museums in the United States and Israel.

The Ultimate Resistance

The ultimate act of resistance for the Jews was simply to preserve their sense of dignity in the dehumanizing environments of the ghettos and camps. The Jewish concept of *Kiddush Hachaim*—the "sanctification of life"—grew out of the horrors of the Holocaust. Since the Nazis intended to annihilate the Jewish people, it became not just a matter of survival but a sacred duty to preserve and enrich one's life and the lives of others. Historian Martin Gilbert captures the essence of spiritual resistance: "Simply to survive was a victory of the human spirit."[32] And despite beatings, torture, and gas chambers, that spirit proved impossible to destroy.

CHAPTER THREE

The Jewish Partisans

Escape attempts from the Holocaust ghettos rarely succeeded. Most attempts ended in death—for those who tried to flee and for other ghetto residents who were murdered in reprisal. Even so, thousands of Jews living in the ghettos of Eastern Europe managed to flee into the surrounding dense forests. There they formed bands of partisans, guerilla fighters who wreaked havoc on German communications lines, train tracks, and power plants. They also helped rescue other Jews from the ghettos and camps. Life as a partisan was difficult. They lived in the forests, exposed to the elements with whatever clothing they were wearing when they fled the ghetto. Foraging for food was a constant problem, as was acquiring weapons and ammunition, which the partisans had to either buy or steal. Friendly villagers sometimes aided the partisans by providing food or shelter. More often, however, the local population offered no help; widespread anti-Semitism and fear of punishment if discovered were strong motivations for doing nothing.

In all, between twenty thousand and thirty thousand Jews escaped the ghettos and camps to become partisans. Whether forming their own groups or joining with existing units, these Jewish partisans displayed great courage and determination in fighting the Nazi regime.

The Partisans of Vilna

During their sweep of Eastern Europe, in June 1941 the Germans captured the Lithuanian city of Vilna, a center of Jewish culture. By September the Nazis had created a ghetto in the city. Some sixty thousand Jews were herded into the ghetto, and by the end of the year the Nazis had murdered about two-thirds of them. One person who survived the massacre was twenty-three-year-old Abba Kovner, a poet and activist in the Vilna underground. When the Germans invaded Vilna, Kovner and a small group of colleagues were hiding in a Dominican convent just outside the city. When Kovner returned to the ghetto he learned of the massacre and concluded that the Nazi menace called for armed resistance. He realized that the murders were just part of the Nazi's plan to exterminate all European Jews.

On January 1, 1942, Kovner gathered together the members of the youth underground and made an impassioned statement. Known as the Vilna Partisan Manifesto, Kovner urged the Jewish youth of Vilna to take up arms against the Nazis.

> "Let us not go like sheep to the slaughter, Jewish youth! . . . Brothers, it is better to die as free fighters than to live at the mercy of killers. Resist, resist, to our last breath."[33]
>
> —Partisan leader Abba Kovner.

Let us not go like sheep to the slaughter, Jewish youth! Do not believe those who are deceiving you. . . . Hitler aimed at destroying the Jews of Europe. It turned out to be the fate of the Jews of Lithuania to be the first. Let us not go like sheep to the slaughter. It is true that we are weak, lacking protection, but the only reply to a murderer is resistance. Brothers, it is better to die as free fighters than to live at the mercy of killers. Resist, resist, to our last breath.[33]

From Vilna, female members of the resistance carried Kovner's call to arms to other ghettos in Eastern Europe.

Into the Forest

Three weeks after the Vilna Partisan Manifesto was announced, Kovner and other underground leaders formed the United Partisan Organization (*Faryenegte Partizaner Organisatsye*, or FPO). The FPO was the first Jewish resistance organization created in a ghetto. Its mission was to prepare for armed action in the event of the liquidation of the ghetto, which they knew could happen at any time. For the next year and a half, FPO members harassed the Germans and spread the word of rebellion to other ghettos.

German officers scan the countryside after capturing the Lithuanian city of Vilna, once a center of Jewish culture. A small group of Jews who escaped the Nazi massacre there formed a partisan organization that conducted many acts of sabotage.

The final liquidation of the Vilna ghetto began on September 23, 1943, when the remaining Jews in the ghetto were killed or deported to labor and extermination camps. Several hundred members of the FPO fled the ghetto through the sewers and escaped to the Rudniki Forest, some 25 miles (40 km) south of Vilna. In the dense woods, other partisans from the Soviet Union, Lithuania, and Poland were already mounting operations against the Germans. Kovner divided his fighters into four battalions with unusual but inspiring names: To Victory, Struggle, Death to Fascism, and, led by Kovner, Avenger. Seeking to acquire more weapons, the Jewish partisans raided local peasant farms and took rifles, pistols, and ammunition by force. It was a dangerous undertaking because of the hatred of the local population toward Jews. The partisans often disguised themselves as Poles or Russians to prevent anti-Semitic locals from identifying them and reporting them to the Germans.

Sabotage

The first mission for the Jewish partisans was the destruction of a German munitions train by blowing up a railroad bridge. After forcing a local peasant to take them to the bridge, the five-person (four men and one woman) raiding party approached the bridge, a wooden structure built over a ravine. After attaching a mine to a support structure and running a detonator cord to the forest, the Jews waited. When the train chugged around a bend and rolled onto the bridge, the mine was detonated. An explosion rang out as the bridge collapsed, plummeting the train into the ravine below. Moments later there were more blasts as the train's cargo of ammunition exploded. The raid was a success, killing fifty Germans as well as destroying the ammunition vital to the *Wehrmacht*.

The Jewish partisans conducted many acts of sabotage over the next years, as recorded in the group's operations diary:

> October 7, 1943: "Destruction of telegraph link. . . . More than 50 telegraph poles were sawn through, the wires were cut and the insulators broken."
>
> December 31, 1943: "A train was blown up on the railroad from Vilna to Grodno. . . . The engine and twenty-one cars carrying troops were derailed. The train had been on its way from Warsaw to Vilna [6 partisans participated, led by Abba Kovner]."
>
> May 10, 1944: "Ambush on the Grodno road. . . . Two units, 'Avenger' and 'To Victory,' took part. Eleven Germans were killed. Booty captured: 6 rifles, 4 hand-grenades, throwers, and 'Degtyarov' machine guns."[34]

Sabotage by Jewish, Soviet, Ukrainian, and other partisans wreaked havoc with the Germans, especially when it came to their most vital supply line, the railroad. As journalist Rich Cohen relates,

"During the peak of the fighting, the Germans lost close to a thousand trains a month to partisans, and millions of dollars' worth of equipment."[35] Tens of thousands of acts of sabotage were undertaken by partisan units, despite the danger and wretched conditions of life in the forests.

Postwar Revenge

The town of Vilna was liberated by the Soviet Army in July 1944, after a fierce five-day battle. Kovner could once more walk the streets of Vilna. Many of his comrades attempted to return to some semblance of an ordinary life, but Kovner saw more struggles ahead. "There will be a time for a normal life," he said. "But that time is not now."[36] After the war Kovner and his Avengers took on a new role: taking revenge, in the name of God, on the Germans who had brutalized and murdered so many Eastern European Jews. In 1946 a plan was devised to poison loaves of bread that would be served to Nazi prisoners being held in detention centers awaiting trial in Nuremburg, Germany, for war crimes. Infiltrating the bakery where the bread was baked, Avenger partisans painted liquid arsenic on three thousand loaves, which were soon delivered to the prison camp. Although it is not known how many deaths the poison caused, more than two thousand Nazis were sickened.

Kovner ultimately grew tired of revenge and, with his partisan wife, Vitka, lived out his days in Palestine. He died in 1987, a hero to the Jewish people.

The Bielski Partisans

Another partisan group was organized in the Eastern European nation of Belarus by three Jewish brothers affected by Nazi atrocities. At the beginning of World War II Belarus was under Soviet control through a pact between Germany and the Soviet Union. When Germany broke that pact in 1941 *Wehrmacht* troops invaded the country, destroying thousands of cities and villages and killing millions of innocent civilians. Among the casualties were the mother, father, and two sons of the Jewish Bielski family. Three surviving sons—Tuvia, Asael, and Zus—fled into the nearby woods, determined to save as many Jews as possible and avenge the deaths of their parents.

Jewish Armed Resistance in Ghettos and Camps, 1941–1944

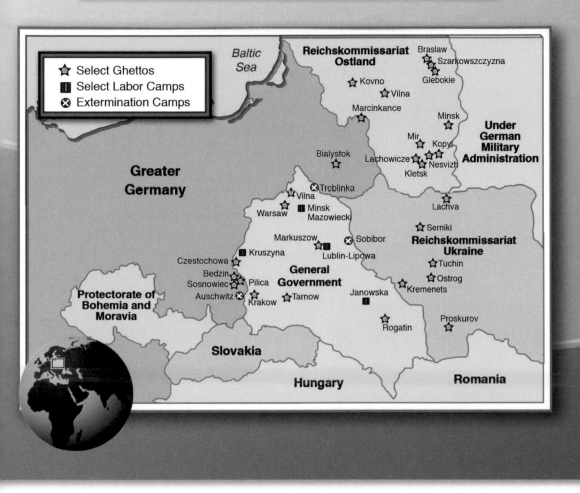

The Bielskis called for other Jews to help form a partisan unit in the forest. At first, few heeded the call. Eventually, however, hundreds more Jews fled to the woods rather than face deportation and death in the Nazi camps. Unlike other partisan organizers in the forest who recruited only refugees fit for combat, the Bielskis welcomed all Jews, including the old, the weak, and the sick. The Bielski unit became a refuge for any Jew who wished to join. Tuvia became the unit's leader, Asael commanded the fighters of the group, and Zus took charge of reconnaissance operations.

Fighting in the Forest

For the next year the partisans led a nomadic existence, moving through the forest to avoid capture by the Germans. The Bielski fighters often collaborated with Soviet partisans on sabotage raids. Tuvia called their first joint raid a "real spiritual high point, that the world should know that there were still Jews alive, and especially Jewish partisans."[37]

In the fall of 1942 a bountiful harvest in Belarus meant that German troops would be well fed during the coming winter. Tuvia and Viktor Pachenko, a Soviet partisan, planned a joint operation to destroy the valuable grain by burning the barns and silos. At midnight on September 1, 1942, two squads of partisans ignited the fires. Sentries had orders to shoot anyone who tried to extinguish the flames.

As flames shot high into the night sky, a fortuitous incident occurred. Soviet bombers, returning from an attack, saw the inferno below and dropped bombs on the burning farms, adding to the destruction. As Pachenko later recalled, "We enjoyed a beautiful show. The bread of the fascists blazed everywhere and the Soviet airplanes droned overhead."[38] Although the bombing was merely a coincidence, it appeared to the Germans that the partisans had formed ties with the Soviet air force. The Germans stepped up their mission to find and destroy the partisans. A bounty of 100,000 *Reichsmarks* (about $40,000 in US currency) was placed on the head of Tuvia Bielski.

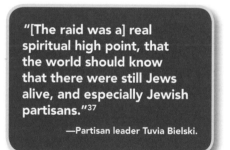

"[The raid was a] real spiritual high point, that the world should know that there were still Jews alive, and especially Jewish partisans."[37]

—Partisan leader Tuvia Bielski.

In the summer of 1943, as German raids came closer to the Bielski camp, Tuvia decided a move was necessary. He told his comrades, "We have to go to a different forest because they have found out we are here. We don't have to be heroes. We just have to live through this war."[39] Heeding their leader's words, the partisans gathered their belongings and began moving east in small groups. Their destination was the Naliboki *puscha*, a dense forest filled with swamps and marshes where few people ever ventured.

Hannah Szenes: Poet and Parachutist

Hungarian-born Hannah Szenes is often remembered for her poetry about Jewish life. But she created an even greater legacy for her daring actions as one of several Jewish members of the British army. After training in Egypt, twenty-two-year-old Szenes volunteered to be part of a group of parachutists dropped into German-occupied Europe. Their mission was to join up with existing partisan units and to provide aid to local Jews.

One of thirty-seven parachutists assigned to the mission, Szenes and two comrades were dropped into Yugoslavia in March 1944. After spending several months with Yugoslavian partisans, Szenes decided to go to her home country of Hungary. However, she was stopped at the border and arrested by Hungarian police. Szenes was taken to a prison in Budapest, where officials attempted to force her to reveal secret partisan radio codes. Despite days of brutal torture, she divulged nothing more than her name. On November 7, 1944, Szenes was executed by a firing squad. She went to her death bravely, refusing a blindfold and never asking for mercy.

The courage and idealism of Hannah Szenes is revealed in her most famous poem. Entitled "Blessed Is the Match," it was written in Yugoslavia, just a few days before her capture.

Blessed is the match that is consumed in kindling flame.

Blessed is the flame that burns in the secret fastness of the heart.

Blessed is the heart with strength to stop its beating for honor's sake.

Blessed is the match that is consumed in kindling flame.

Quoted in Marie Syrkin, *Blessed Is the Match*. Philadelphia: Jewish Publication Society of America, 1976, p. 24.

A New Camp

Deep in the *puscha* the partisans built an elaborate base of operations; their group now numbered about seven hundred Jews. In the relative safety of the forest living quarters were constructed, each holding between twenty and forty partisans. Support structures went up, including a kitchen, bakery, mill, tannery, and hospital. Workshops with skilled artisans such as carpenters, tailors, shoemakers, and metal workers produced whatever necessities the partisans needed.

The Bielski partisans continued their sabotage raids, mining railroads and destroying bridges and telephone lines. They also skirmished with German troops and took revenge on local villagers who had killed Jews or collaborated with the Nazis. But to Tuvia, even more important than killing Germans was providing protection for his band of Jewish refugees. "I'd rather save one old Jewish woman," he once said, "than kill ten German soldiers."[40] When Soviet commanders tried to combine the Bielski unit with their partisan forces, Tuvia insisted on keeping undivided control of his unit. By mid-1944, when the Soviet Red Army liberated the Naliboki *puscha*, the Bielskis

An illustration from around 1943 depicts a group of Russian partisans capturing a German soldier. Groups of partisans, some Jewish and some not, joined together in a common cause: to defeat the Nazis.

had destroyed countless Nazi war supplies and killed 381 Germans. But even more important to the Bielskis was the fact that they had saved the lives of twelve hundred Jews in the partisan camp.

Jewish Family Camps

Around the time the partisans were building up their fighting units, another movement was taking place in the forests of Eastern Europe. In 1942, as German troops massacred Jews in raids on towns and villages, those who could escaped to nearby woods. There they formed family camps. These camps provided a hiding place and some measure of protection for those who had fled the Nazi terror. Some camps consisted of one or two families, while others provided a refuge for hundreds of Jews.

Members of the family camps experienced many of the same hardships as the forest-dwelling partisans. They struggled to build shelters and find food. Each family camp had a contingent of armed men who raided farms and villages for food. This created hostility toward the Jews of the family camps among the local peasants, who were already inclined toward anti-Semitism. Raiding parties often encountered armed peasants who fought back. Angered farmers sometimes led local police to the location of a family camp, resulting in arrests or the murder of the camp's inhabitants. This hostility also caused conflict with the Soviet partisans who relied on the same peasants for their own food supplies. In the early stages of the partisan operations in the forests, the Soviets often raided the family camps. They took money, clothing, and weapons—leaving the family camps defenseless. As the Soviet partisans became more organized, however, they sometimes provided protection for the family camps. In many cases the family camps provided services—such as repairing weapons—for the partisans.

On the Move

The security of living in a family camp did not always last. The Germans organized frequent manhunts in the forests to root out partisan guerillas and Jewish refugees. To keep ahead of the advancing soldiers the family camps had to move frequently. Because the

The Jewish Army in France

While many Jewish partisans were conducting clandestine operations in the nations of Eastern Europe, France had its share of partisan fighters harassing the country's German occupiers. One group, the Armée Juive, or Jewish Army, was established in 1942 in Vichy, France. Vichy was the government of the southern part of France that, while not occupied by Germany, collaborated with the Nazis.

The Jewish Army was composed of members of the Zionist youth movement, a group dedicated to Jewish nationalism in Palestine. Those who joined the Army took the following oath:

"Placing my right hand on the blue and white flag

I swear fidelity to the Jewish Army

And obedience to its leaders.

May my people live again

May Eretz-Israel [the Jewish state] be reborn

Liberty or death."

The primary goal of the Jewish Army was the smuggling of Jews to neutral Spain; from there, the refugees made their way to Palestine. Other objectives included sabotaging German military assets such as trains and trucks, providing hiding places for French Jews, and supporting the creation of a Jewish state in Palestine. As more underground organizations joined forces with the Jewish Army, it changed its name to the Jewish Fighting Organization (OJC). By 1944 the group had grown to about two thousand members. As Allied forces pushed into France the OJC participated in the liberation of many cities, including Toulouse, Nice, Lyon, and Paris.

Quoted in The Museum of the Jewish Soldier in World War 2, "France." www.jwmww2 .org.

family camps included children, the infirm, and the elderly, moving from place to place in the forest proved difficult. A member of a family camp describes their trek to a new campsite in the Borisov Forest of Belarus.

> Every day we could expect to be attacked. We received information that the Germans had been informed of our whereabouts. . . . We packed our things, loaded our rucksacks, folded our blankets on top, and set out on our way. . . . We had to walk kilometers upon kilometers. . . . Our feet got stuck in the mud. . . . Everything was damp and wet. . . . In this manner, we crossed forests, fields, and paths until we reached the Borisov Forest.[41]

Upon reaching their destination, guards were posted, living accommodations begun, and raiders sent out to get food. No one knew when they would be forced to pack up and move again. Besides the rigors of traveling, exposure to the elements, especially in the winter months, took a toll on the family camps. Diseases such as typhus ran through many of the camps, which had no medicine to treat the afflicted.

"Every day we could expect to be attacked. . . . We packed our things, loaded our rucksacks, folded our blankets on top, and set out on our way. . . . We had to walk kilometers upon kilometers. . . . Our feet got stuck in the mud. . . . Everything was damp and wet."[41]

—Family camp member.

Although there are no reliable statistics concerning the family camps, it is estimated that around ten thousand Jews were saved from the Nazis by escaping to the forest encampments. Thousands more were likely saved by the actions of the partisans who battled the Germans in a war of stealth fighting and guerilla tactics. Without uniforms, airplanes, or tanks, the Jewish partisans played a vital role in defeating the Third Reich.

CHAPTER FOUR

Saving the Children

On the nights of November 9 and 10, 1938, troops of the Nazi *Sturmabteilung* (Storm Detachment) carried out a vicious assault against Jews in Germany, Austria, and parts of Czechoslovakia. Bands of storm troopers roamed the streets of towns and cities, setting synagogues on fire and destroying businesses owned by Jews. Local authorities, warned by the Nazis not to interfere, looked on in silence. By the next morning some five hundred synagogues had been demolished, smoke from the burning buildings filling the air. At least ninety Jews were killed and thirty thousand sent to concentration camps. The streets, littered with glass shards from thousands of broken shop windows, sparkled like crystal, giving the incident the name *Kristallnacht* ("crystal night," or, more popularly, "night of broken glass.")

Kristallnacht marked a turning point in the Nazi oppression of Jews. Before that fateful night, the Nazis tried to provoke Jews to leave Germany and the occupied territories by systematic persecution and intimidation. Now, however, the Jews realized that their very lives were in danger. Of all the Jews, children were the most vulnerable. Relocation was difficult for families, as few nations were willing to ease their restrictions on Jewish immigration. But if the adults could not flee, they could try to somehow get their children to safety.

Many individuals and organizations stepped forward to rescue the children of the Holocaust. Risking their lives, they helped get Jewish children out of Nazi-controlled territory or hide children who could not escape. Their actions are examples of compassion and bravery in a time of terror and death.

The *Kindertransport*

The world was shocked by the *Kristallnacht* violence committed by the Nazis against the Jews. US president Franklin Delano Roosevelt proclaimed that he "could scarcely believe that such things could occur in a twentieth century civilization."[42] But such sentiment did not always translate into action. Most nations refused to increase their quotas for Jewish immigration, citing fear of German reprisals or anti-Semitic backlash among friendly nations. The exception was Great Britain.

Passersby look at shops that were destroyed in 1938 during Kristallnacht, a wave of violent attacks on property and businesses owned by Jews. This event, which marked a new level of Nazi aggression toward Jews, sparked efforts to get Jewish children out of Nazi-controlled territory.

Shortly after *Kristallnacht* groups of Jewish, Christian, and Quaker refugee workers formed an association called the Movement for the Care of Children from Germany. They petitioned the British Parliament to allow Jewish refugee children into the country. After debating the desperate situation of Europe's Jews, Parliament agreed to allow refugee children under seventeen years of age to enter Britain. British home secretary Samuel Hoare said at the time, "Here is a chance of taking a young generation of a great people, here is a chance of mitigating to some extent the terrible suffering of their parents and their friends."[43]

The effort to bring young Jews to safety in Britain operated with certain conditions. The costs of the children's care, education, and eventual return to their homelands were to be paid by sponsoring organizations or individuals. The children could only bring what they could carry onto the trains and ferries that would transport them to safety. And, perhaps the most difficult condition of all, they would have to leave their parents behind. At the time, it was thought that Nazi persecution of the Jews would be over quickly and that the children could soon be reunited with their families.

> "Here is a chance of taking a young generation of a great people, here is a chance of mitigating to some extent the terrible suffering of their parents and their friends."[43]
>
> —British home secretary Samuel Hoare.

Leaving the Reich

After receiving approval from the British government, the Movement for the Care of Children from Germany sent members to Germany to work out the details of the plan, which would come to be known as the *Kindertransport* (children's transport). German officials did not oppose the arrangement, as long as the children did not take anything of value with them. A request was broadcast over England's BBC radio network for foster families to accept the children upon arrival. Volunteers compiled lists of eligible children, concentrating first on those at immediate risk: children in concentration camps, orphans, and those who might soon be deported to the camps.

The first *Kindertransport* train departed from Berlin on December 1, 1938. Parents gathered on the platform to say good-bye to their

The Hiding Place

As a child, Jaap Sitters, a Dutch Jew, sometimes had to sleep in a cramped opening under the floor of his house. His parents sent him there when they heard that German soldiers were nearby. Years later Sitters recalled his feelings while in hiding.

There was a space around thirty inches beneath the floor that might work as a place to hide. . . . There was just enough room to lie down in the sand, but you couldn't even crouch in there. . . . When I was getting ready for bed [my father] said, "You'd better sleep in the hiding place this evening." The thought of it made me shiver, but I didn't dare admit that. I slid into the hiding place an hour later, carrying a woolen blanket. Feet first, then the rest of me. It wasn't easy.

Finally I was in position. The hatch went down. The wooden floor was directly above my nose. I lay there in the sand, wrapped up in my blanket. It was pitch-dark. For a while I could still hear muffled voices. Then nothing.

I woke up some time in the night. It was cold. As soon as I remembered where I was, I started to panic. The sand was so wet. I heard someone screaming, and I realized it was me. I flew out of the hiding place. There was no one in the living room. I tiptoed back to my own bed, where I shivered with cold as I waited for the night to end.

Quoted in Marcel Prins and Peter Henk Steenhuis, *Hidden Like Anne Frank: 14 True Stories of Survival.* New York: Arthur A. Levine, 2011, pp. 31–32.

children, not knowing if they would ever see them again. Teenager Alexander Gordon, who was one of the first *Kindertransport* children, describes the scene in a 2000 documentary film.

I reported to the train at six o'clock in the morning with one suitcase, ten marks [German currency], and very skimpy clothing. The station was crowded with children of all ages, from four to seventeen, and their parents. I think there must have been three hundred of us. . . . The people were behind the gates and the parents were telling the small children to get on to the train. The children didn't want to leave. The parents said "We'll see you in England in a few weeks," and there was crying and it was bedlam.[44]

The *Kindertransport* trains traveled across Germany to a port city in the Netherlands or Belgium. There the children boarded a ferry to sail to Harwich, England. It was a relatively short trip, and the first group of children to leave Germany landed in England on December 2.

Strangers in a Strange Land

Not all the children had sponsors waiting for them upon their arrival. Those for whom volunteer sponsors had been arranged traveled by rail to London to meet their new families. Children without sponsors were sent to special camps until they were taken in by foster families or relocated to group homes or hostels.

> "The people were behind the gates and the parents were telling the small children to get on to the train. The children didn't want to leave. The parents said 'We'll see you in England in a few weeks,' and there was crying and it was bedlam."[44]
>
> —*Kindertransport* child Alexander Gordon.

Life in their new homeland was difficult for the Jewish children. The climate and food in England was different and unfamiliar to the children. Living with strange families, not knowing the language or customs of their sponsors, and being separated from their friends and families caused great anxiety among many of the *Kindertransport* children. *Kindertransport* refugee Lorraine Allard recalls that her foster parents "were completely different from my family. They had an unhappy marriage. . . . They were kind to me. They were as kind as they were to their son. But affection didn't exist in the house."[45] Eventually, most of the children began adapting to their new surroundings. They went to school and began learning English. Many were able to write letters to their real families, but for some, the memories of their past lives began to fade.

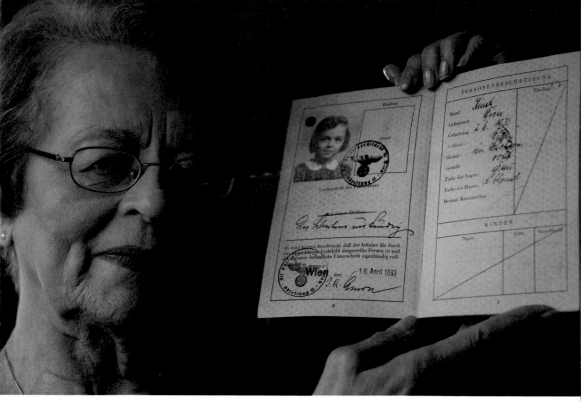

Eve Willman holds a copy of her 1939 German passport. Willman was among the thousands of Jewish children who escaped the Nazi genocide thanks to the Kindertransport, which brought them to England.

The *Kindertransport* ended on September 1, 1939, when Germany's invasion of Poland ignited World War II. By that time some ten thousand young people (most of whom were Jews) had been rescued from the ravages of the Holocaust.

Hiding the Children

Although the *Kindertransport* saved thousands of lives, it could not accommodate every Jewish child in Eastern Europe. Millions of children were left behind when the war broke out. With no chance of removing them from the growing Nazi menace, another way to protect the children had to be found.

Providing hiding places for Jewish children was one effective, though dangerous, method to safeguard them. Some children could hide in plain sight, attending school and living in the open. Many of these children were given non-Jewish names by their Christian foster families and adopted a Christian way of life to protect them from anti-Semitism.

Janusz Korczak: Leading the Children

Janusz Korczak was a Jewish educator, writer, and doctor in Warsaw. He devoted his life to children, applying his studies in child psychology to his educational activities. In 1912 Korczak established an orphanage for Jewish children in Warsaw; he called it *Dom Seriot* (Orphan House). There children lived and learned in an environment of mutual respect.

When the Nazis established the Warsaw ghetto in 1940, *Dom Seriot* ended up on the Aryan side of the barricades separating the ghetto from the rest of Warsaw. Korczak and his nearly two hundred orphans were forced to move to a building inside the ghetto. The move changed nothing for Korczak; he continued to do whatever he could to keep the children safe and fed.

Several times the Warsaw underground offered Korczak means to escape the ghetto; each time he refused to abandon his orphans. The end came on August 5, 1942, when the Nazis rounded up the orphans and their teachers and led them to the *Umschlagplatz* for deportation to Treblinka. Korczak silently marched at the head of the procession, as Emanuel Ringelblum records in his diary: "This was not a march to the railway cars, this was an organized, wordless protest against the murder! . . . The children marched in rows of four, with Korczak leading them, looking straight ahead, and holding a child's hand on each side." Even on the march to certain death, Janusz Korczak did not abandon his children.

Quoted in Marilyn J. Harran and John Roth, "Janusz Korczak," in *The Holocaust Chronicle*. Lincolnwood, IL: Publications International, 2000, p. 348.

Others were hidden out of harm's way in monasteries, convents, orphanages, or private homes. Attics, closets, and cramped spaces under floorboards all served as refuges for the hidden children when Germans came to search for Jews. Children who were sent to farms often lived in haylofts to avoid detection. Although most of the adults were kind to the young Jews in their custody, there were incidents of abuse. Some guardians forced the children to work long hours or take on laborious chores around the house.

It was a frightening and confusing time for Europe's young Jewish population. The normal exuberance of youth had to be restrained for fear that any noise would lead to discovery. Many of the youngest could not understand what was happening or why they were separated from their families. Older children realized the danger they were in and lived with constant anxiety. For the hidden children it was a time of lost youth and forgotten innocence.

The Village That Saved Children

One of the most remarkable rescues of the Holocaust occurred because an entire village, inhabited by people with a history of opposing religious persecution, agreed to become a refuge for Jewish children. Between the sixteenth and eighteenth centuries the Vivarais Plateau in southern France was a refuge for religiously oppressed Christians known as Huguenots. Persecuted by the Roman Catholic Church, the Huguenots found freedom to live and worship as they pleased in the villages and farms of this region. Throughout the years that followed, the descendants of the Huguenots have lived and farmed in peace on the plateau, never forgetting what it was like for their forebears to be an oppressed minority.

Le Chambon-sur-Lignon, the largest village on the Vivarais Plateau, played an important role in rescuing Jewish children during World War II. When Hitler conquered France in 1940, Jews from the occupied northern part of the country began fleeing to the unoccupied south, seeking refuge in places like Le Chambon. The village's Protestant minister André Trocmé became aware of the situation when Jewish refugees began arriving in Le Chambon. Trocmé preached to his congregation about the responsibilities of Christians to help those in need. Soon the entire population of Le Chambon-sur-Lignon voiced its willingness to help.

Finding Sanctuary

Trocmé and his assistant minister, Edouard Theis, led the effort to turn the Vivarais Plateau into a sanctuary for refugees. Other smaller villages followed the lead of Le Chambon. As the war progressed, trains and buses carrying young refugees arrived daily in Le Chambon and other villages on the plateau. The Oeuvre de Secours aux Enfants (OSE, or Children's Relief Works), a Jewish children's welfare organization, helped place children in private or group homes. Other organizations, including the Swiss Red Cross and the Salvation Army, and even friendly governments such as Sweden, contributed funds to support the children.

> "None of us thought that we were heroes. We were just people trying to do our best."[47]
>
> —Magda Trocmé, wife of pastor at Le Chambon-sur-Lignon.

In Le Chambon the children lived with families in boardinghouses or group homes or on farms. They went to school every day and made new friends. Those children who did not speak French took language lessons. Many refugee children joined Boy Scout and Girl Scout troops in the village. These types of activities made life seem almost normal. Henri, nine years old at the time of his rescue, described his life in Le Chambon in a 2004 interview. (Henri's account appears in a 2007 book; the authors of that book changed the interview to present tense to appear as though nine-year-old Henri is speaking. Their version appears here.)

> There's lots to do here. We go on hikes in the woods and pick mushrooms and berries, but we don't eat the mushrooms. . . . We're learning Scout things, like tying knots and wilderness survival. We play ball games and annoy the girls. Sometimes it's fun here, but the fear is always there in the pit of my stomach. I have to be careful of everything I say and do. I feel so alone all the time.[46]

Henri's fear was not without reason: Even on the plateau, French *gendarmes* (policemen) and German troops conducted periodic searches for Jews. On June 29, 1943, eighteen students were dragged from the Maison des Roches boarding school in Le Chambon, interrogated, and then arrested and deported. Only seven survived the war, five died at Auschwitz, and six were never accounted for. Their teacher, Trocmé's cousin, was sent to the Majdanek killing center, where he died in April 1944.

In August 1944 France was liberated from its Nazi oppressors. An estimated three thousand to five thousand refugees, both children and adults, had been saved from harm. Trocmé's wife, Magda, later commented, "None of us thought that we were heroes. We were just people trying to do our best."[47] Many of the children, now grown, held reunions in later years to remember their wartime experiences and honor the compassionate people of Le Chambon-sur-Lignon and the other villages on the Vivarais Plateau.

The Angel of Warsaw

Far away from France, on a dark night in the Warsaw ghetto in 1942, a young woman gently laid a six-month-old child named Elzbieta in a wooden carpenter's toolbox. Drugged so as not to make a sound, the baby was placed next to a silver spoon engraved with her name and the date she was born—the only birth certificate Elzbieta would ever have. The woman put the box on a truck loaded with bricks that was headed out of the ghetto toward the Aryan, or non-Jewish, side of Warsaw. In that truck Elzbieta was carried to safety and into the arms of the couple she would come to know as her parents. The woman who arranged the rescue of little Elzbieta was Irena Sendler, a thirty-two-year-old Roman Catholic social worker who was responsible for saving some twenty-five hundred Jewish children from the Warsaw ghetto.

Born in 1910, Sendler was living in Warsaw when the Germans invaded Poland. From the beginning of the German occupation, Sendler helped the Jews by operating cafeterias for the poor, elderly, and orphaned, and by providing families with false identification papers to protect them from Nazi persecution.

When Zegota—code name for the Council to Aid Jews—was established by the Polish underground in October 1942, Sendler became head of the group's Children's Section. A pass from the Warsaw Epidemic Control Department allowed her free access to the ghetto. Wearing a nurse's uniform, Sendler was able to enter the ghetto on the pretext of medical missions. She was shocked by the conditions in the ghetto, especially for the children. She began to devise ways for getting the children out of the ghetto. She smuggled some children out in gunnysacks or wooden crates, while others were hidden in body bags or even coffins. Once outside the ghetto, the children were

A playful group of children, oblivious to the dangers around them, pose for a photographer at a Polish convent in 1943. The children were rescued from the Warsaw ghetto by a thirty-two-year-old Roman Catholic social worker named Irena Sendler.

given false identities and placed with foster parents, orphanages, or convents. Sendler wrote down the real names of all the children she rescued. She hid the names in glass jars that she buried in the hope that one day the children would find this information and use it to reunite with their real families.

Captured by the Nazis

In 1943 the Nazis learned of Sendler's activities and arrested her. Sent to Pawiak prison in Warsaw, she was tortured by the Nazis, who broke her legs and feet. But Sendler did not reveal the names of the families protecting the children she had freed. Sentenced to death, Sendler was saved from a firing squad and set free by the last-minute bribe of a guard. She continued her rescue activities under an assumed name.

After the war Sendler dug up the jars and gave the information to Zegota. Although some children were reunited with their families, most of their parents and grandparents had been killed during the war. When later asked what motivated her, Sendler replied, "I was brought up to believe that a person must be rescued when drowning, regardless of religion and nationality."[48] For her selfless actions, Sendler was called the "Angel of Warsaw." To the children she saved, she truly was a guardian angel.

Resuming Life

During years of hiding from the Nazis, many Jewish children became adjusted to the new and different life that had been imposed upon them. When the war ended in 1945, these rescued children were finally free to resume their former lives. For many of them, however, those lives no longer existed. The war and the Nazi killing centers had taken most of their parents' lives, leaving them orphans with no one to take care of them. Those who were able to rejoin their families often found the reunion difficult. Children who had spent years in hiding were older now and often very different people than their parents remembered. Rescued babies and toddlers had no memory at all of their real parents and were frightened by their separation from the only families they had ever known.

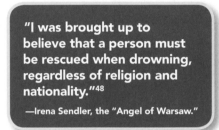

"I was brought up to believe that a person must be rescued when drowning, regardless of religion and nationality."[48]

—Irena Sendler, the "Angel of Warsaw."

And yet, they had survived. About 1.2 million Jewish children perished during the Holocaust. Although the children who lived are but a small fraction of that number (6 to 11 percent by one estimate), their survival proved that the Nazi plan to destroy the future of the Jewish race had failed.

CHAPTER FIVE

The Righteous Among the Nations

Maria Zurawska was not expecting visitors when three desperate people arrived at her house in the summer of 1943. The Jewish strangers—Helen Haber; her mother, Gittel; and Helen's five-year-old daughter, Julia—had escaped from the Zlochow ghetto in Poland and sought refuge at the first house they encountered. Little Julia was sick and in urgent need of medical attention.

Zurawska did not hesitate. She took the three in, sheltering them and nursing Julia back to health. When German soldiers came to Zurawska's house looking for Jews, she gave them misleading information. Then she fled with her own children and the three Jewish refugees to a nearby village. There they remained safe until the end of the war.

In a ceremony on January 16, 2014, Zurawska received a posthumous honor for rescuing her three Jewish visitors. She was acknowledged as one of the "Righteous Among the Nations," an honor given to gentiles (non-Jews) who saved Jewish lives during the Holocaust. The recognition was bestowed by Yad Vashem, the official Jewish Holocaust memorial. Zurawska joined the more than twenty-four thousand people from forty-seven countries who have been so recognized since 1963.

The Righteous are a diverse group that includes Christians and Muslims, diplomats and businessmen, managers and laborers, royalty and commoners. Most, like Zurawska, were simply ordinary people risking their lives to do what was right in a dangerous world. In doing so, they embodied the spirit expressed in Jewish tradition: "Whoever saves a life, it is considered as if he saved the entire world."[49]

Oskar Schindler: From Spy to Savior

The gentiles who risked their lives protecting Jews came from varied backgrounds and all walks of life. For many of them, doing whatever they could to help someone in need seemed to come naturally. But almost no one who knew Oskar Schindler would have predicted that one day he would rescue hundreds of Jews during the Holocaust. Born in 1908 in Zwittau, Czechoslovakia (now the Czech Republic), Schindler grew up to enjoy wild parties, heavy drinking, and expensive cars. He thought nothing of illegally buying and selling on the black market or cheating on his wife. But he was also responsible for saving the lives of twelve hundred Jews during the Holocaust.

A salesman by trade, Schindler's outgoing personality and charm gave him a unique ability to make contacts that were helpful in his business dealings. That same ability drew the notice of the *Abwehr* (German military intelligence agency), which recruited him to collect information on Polish military activities in preparation for the German invasion of Poland. Although he was now a Nazi spy, Schindler's pri-

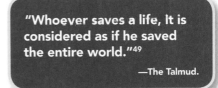

"Whoever saves a life, It is considered as if he saved the entire world."[49]

—The Talmud.

mary interest was business, and like many German businessmen he saw that the war created an opportunity for making money. He moved to Krakow, the capital of German-occupied Poland, seeking a business he could buy or invest in. Ideally, it would be a firm that could do business with the German military, which would assure its success. He found a bankrupt company called Rekord, which had manufactured enamel-coated pots, pans, and kitchen utensils. By December 1939 Schindler had leased the company and renamed it Deutsche Emalwarenfabrik Oskar Schindler, known informally as Emalia.

The *Schindlerjuden*

A business cannot run without personnel, and Schindler recruited Polish workers for his new factory. But he knew that the less he paid his employees, the more profit he would make. He began hiring Jews for Emalia because the Nazis mandated that they be paid less than Poles. By their labor, these *Schindlerjuden*, or Schindler Jews, helped make him a rich man, the goal that he had aspired to on his arrival in Krakow. As the Nazi treatment of Jews in the city worsened, Schindler experienced a gradual change of heart. He would ultimately spend all his wealth protecting the Jews of Krakow.

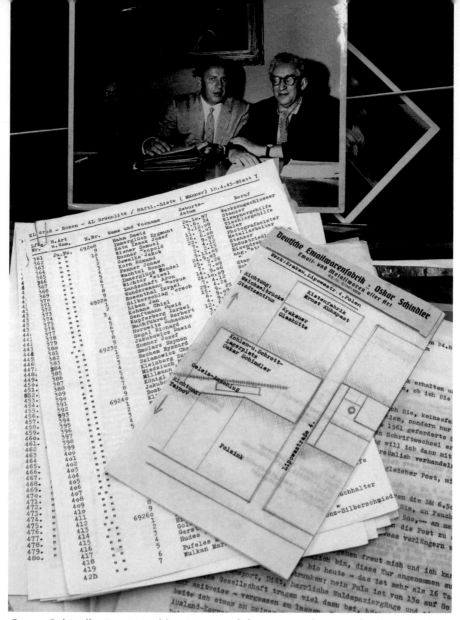

Oscar Schindler's original list (pictured) has more than twelve hundred names on it. Schindler saved hundreds of Polish Jews by giving them jobs in his factories. Schindler appears in the center of the photo above.

In March 1941 the Nazis established a ghetto in Krakow. Each day Schindler's Jewish employees walked to his factory from the ghetto. Schindler tried to make life better for his workers. At Emalia, workers had access to a medical clinic and an employee dining room. "Those who worked in Schindler's factory were truly privileged," recalls Moshe Bejski, a former *Schindlerjude*. "Not only did he spend his own money to supply them with extra food, but he also took care of hundreds of their everyday problems, and provided the workers with medicine, clothing, and even eyeglasses."[50]

While Schindler was helping his Jewish workers, the Nazis were moving forward with their plan to eliminate them. The Krakow ghetto was liquidated in March 1943. Jews who were able to work, including several hundred Emalia workers, were sent to a labor camp in nearby Plaszow. Schindler bribed camp officials to prevent them from relocating his workers to extermination camps. But in the summer of 1944, when Schindler learned the Nazis were about to liquidate Plaszow, he devised a new plan to save the Jews.

The Lists

Schindler requested permission from the Nazis to build a new munitions factory in the city of Brünnlitz, in his home country of Czechoslovakia. The factory, and an adjacent camp to house his workers, would employ about eleven hundred Jews and be financed with Schindler's own money. After permission was granted, Schindler supervised the creation of a list of Jews to be transferred to the new factory. Jews who were not on the list were sent from Plaszow to their deaths at Auschwitz. Two lists were drawn up in the fall of 1944: a men's list with seven hundred names, and a women's list bearing three hundred names. Later, several revisions were made, and other Jews were added to the final lists.

In October 1944 trains carrying seven hundred men arrived at Brünnlitz after a stop at the Gross-Rosen concentration camp. A train with three hundred women had been routed first to Auschwitz but had not yet arrived at Brünnlitz. When Schindler was informed of this, he used his influence, along with huge bribes, to make sure his female workers were quickly transported to Brünnlitz. For the next five months Schindler's new factory produced ammunition that was purposely defective so as not to aid the German war effort.

After the War

When Germany surrendered in May 1945, Schindler gathered his workers for a final, farewell speech, during which he said, "It was always my will to demonstrate and defend humanity, to conduct my affairs humanely, the principle that guided all of my decisions."[51] Schindler left Brünnlitz the next day. His fortune was gone, but the lives of twelve hundred Jews would forever be his legacy.

In a 1964 interview Schindler spoke humbly about why he helped the Jews. "I just couldn't stand by and see people destroyed. I did what I could, what I had to do, what my conscience told me I must do. That's all there is to it."[52] By his actions, Oskar Schindler was posthumously honored as one of the Righteous Among the Nations in 1993.

Miep Gies and the Secret Annex

Schindler's flamboyant personality helped him save the Jewish workers in his factory. But not all of the Righteous were so bold. In Amsterdam, the Netherlands, an ordinary woman and her husband kept a Jewish family safe in hiding for almost two years.

The Germans invaded the Netherlands on May 10, 1940, and within four days they had occupied the country. This was troubling for Jewish businessman Otto Frank. He had moved his family—his wife Edith and daughters Margot and Anne—from Germany to Amsterdam in 1933 as Hitler gained power in Europe. As Frank's business, called Opekta, grew over the next few years, so did Nazi persecution of Jews in the Netherlands. In early 1942 Frank devised a plan to protect his family: They would go into hiding in an annex behind the Opekta offices. He approached his thirty-three-year-old secretary and close friend, Austrian-born Miep Gies. "I have a secret to confide in you," he said. "Edith, Margot, Anne, and I are planning to go under—to go into hiding. . . . Miep, are you willing to take on the responsibility of taking care of us while we are in hiding?"[53] Without hesitation she agreed to help the Franks, knowing that the punishment for hiding Jews was death.

Otto Frank planned to take his family and several friends to the annex on July 16, 1942. But on July 5 a notice was delivered ordering Margot to report to the German authorities for relocation to a concentration camp—a sure death sentence. The Nazis had forced Otto's hand: The Franks would have to go into hiding the next day.

The refugees occupied the top two floors and attic of the annex. The cramped rooms sheltered eight people: the Franks; their friends Hermann and Auguste van Pels and their son, Peter; and Fritz Pfeffer. For two years this secret annex was the entire world for the eight Jews. They dared not leave their hiding place, so whatever

Varian Fry: An American Schindler

On a visit to Berlin in 1935 American journalist Varian Fry was disturbed by what he saw. The persecution of Jews in the early stages of the Third Reich motivated him to write newspaper articles detailing Nazi atrocities. But merely writing about it was not enough. "I could not remain idle as long as I had any chances at all of saving even a few of its intended victims," Fry later said.

In June 1940 a group of Americans formed the Emergency Rescue Committee to liberate Jewish intellectuals from German-controlled Vichy, France. A list of two hundred people was drawn up, and thirty-two-year-old Fry was assigned to lead the rescue operation. With $3,000 and no experience in covert action, Fry arrived in France on August 15, 1940. Settling into a hotel in Marseille, he immediately began contacting the people on the list. Soon Fry and his staff were interviewing up to seventy people a day to determine who was in the most danger. Refugees were spirited out of harm's way by rail, boat, and over land to such safe countries as Spain, Portugal, Cuba, and the United States.

Although initially planning to spend one month in France, Fry's mission lasted a year. The original list of two hundred grew into a massive operation that ultimately saved as many as two thousand refugees. Fry died in 1967 and was posthumously designated Righteous Among the Nations in 1994.

Quoted in Mordecai Paldiel, *Saving the Jews: Amazing Stories of Men and Women Who Defied the "Final Solution."* Rockville, MD: Schreiber, 2000, p. 60.

they needed—food, clothing, reading material, and news from the outside world—had to be brought to them. Each morning, Miep Gies went to the secret annex. "I, early in the morning," she recalls, "would be the first to visit, the first face after a long night locked in together. But this visit was business only, to get the list for groceries, see what was needed for the day."[54] Purchasing large amounts of groceries could have brought suspicion on Gies. "I was shopping for seven [later eight] people in hiding as well as for [husband Jan] and myself. Often I had to go to several shops to get the quantities I needed, but I wasn't particularly conspicuous. These were not normal times."[55] Outside the annex in the streets of Amsterdam, Jews were being dragged from their homes and deported to labor or extermination camps.

Discovery

Gies was working in her office on August 4, 1944, when Gestapo (German Secret State Police) officers opened the door. They had been given a tip that Jews were being hidden somewhere in Opekta. Gies and her coworkers sat terrified as the officers searched the building, finally discovering the entrance to the secret annex. All of the hidden Jews were arrested and taken away. Gies later went up to the annex, walking through empty, ransacked rooms. In the Franks' bedroom she paused. "On the floor," Gies recalls, "amidst the chaos of papers and books, my eye lit on the little red-orange checkered, cloth-bound diary that Anne had received from her father on her thirteenth birthday." She took the diary and put it in her desk drawer, thinking at the time, "I'll keep everything safe for Anne until she comes back."[56]

> "I am not a hero. . . . I willingly did what I could to help. My husband did as well. It was not enough."[57]
>
> —Miep Gies, Dutch hider of the Anne Frank family.

Anne never came back. She died from typhus in the Bergen-Belsen concentration camp. She was fifteen years old. But her words live on in the diary that Gies kept safe. Otto Frank, the only one of the eight to survive, published his daughter's diary in June 1947 as *The Secret Annex*—later to be known around the world as *The Diary*

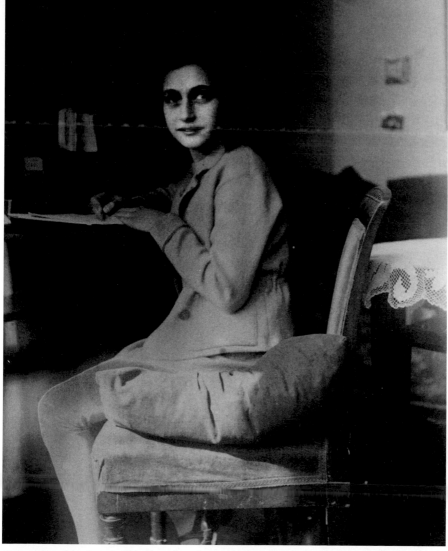

Anne Frank, pictured in her family's Amsterdam apartment before they went into hiding, began her famous diary here. The family was eventually discovered. Anne Frank died in the Bergen-Belsen concentration camp, but her words live on.

of Anne Frank. Since then millions of people have been moved by the innermost thoughts of a girl caught up in the horrors of the Holocaust. Had Gies not kept the diary safe, it likely would have been destroyed by the Nazis.

In 1977 Miep Gies and her husband were declared "Righteous Among the Nations." Despite the honor, Gies remained humble. Ten years later she wrote, "I am not a hero. . . . I willingly did what I could to help. My husband did as well. It was not enough."[57]

The Danish Underground

Most of those honored as the Righteous Among the Nations are individual people such as Oskar Schindler and Miep Gies, who acted alone and in extraordinary ways. But one group has also been given this honor. The fighters of the Danish underground risked their lives to coordinate the escape of nearly all their Jewish countrymen—a number totaling nearly eight thousand people. For their selfless actions, they too have been named the Righteous Among the Nations.

The German occupation of Denmark, which began with an invasion on April 9, 1940, was different than that of other European nations. Realizing that the small Danish army was no match for Hitler's *Wehrmacht*, King Christian X surrendered his nation two hours after

People who took extraordinary steps to save Jews during the Holocaust have been recognized by Israel as the Righteous Among the Nations. One of these is Andree Geulen-Herscovici of Belgium (pictured), who helped hide Jewish children with Christian families and at monasteries over a period of two years.

the invasion began. At the time, about seventy-seven hundred Jews lived in Denmark—and all were well-assimilated into Danish society. At first the Nazis were lenient toward Denmark's Jews. They did not force them into ghettos, and the Jews did not have to wear the yellow Star of David, which was required of Jews throughout Nazi Germany and the Nazi-occupied territories. But that tolerance changed as clandestine raids by the Danish resistance increased.

Sailing to Safety

By August 1943 sabotage by Danish underground fighters had become so destructive to the Nazis that they imposed martial law in Denmark. Their next step, the deportation of all the Jews in Denmark, was scheduled to begin on October 1. Word of the Nazi plan was leaked to the Danish government, and when the roundup began the Nazis found only 284 Jews (subsequent raids would raise the total to 474). The rest had been hidden by Danish citizens or were being transported to safety in neutral Sweden. Historian Leni Yahil describes the Jews as disappearing "behind a living wall raised by the Danish people in the space of one night."[58]

Sweden's government, appalled by the Nazi action in Denmark, announced that their country would provide a safe haven for any Jews who escaped from Denmark. The way to safety was to cross the Øresund Strait, a 2.5- to 15-mile-wide channel (4 to 24 km) that separates Denmark from Sweden. The Danish underground began organizing crossings as early as September 28, arranging for fishermen to transport groups of Jews across the strait. The fishermen required payment from the Jews for their services; money was raised by Danish relief organizations for those who could not afford the fees. Dr. Jørgen Gersfelt, who helped bring Jews to the boats, recalls the ferrying of the Jewish refugees.

> All motorboats that were able to navigate maintained a regular service between Snekkersten and the Kobbervaerkshavnen harbor in Helsingborg [Sweden]. The Jews arrived by train and car, carrying heavy suitcases and small children in their arms, and piled into the boats that were waiting for them with their engines running.[59]

A Japanese Rescuer

On December 7, 1941, the Japanese attack on Pearl Harbor placed that nation squarely on the side of the Axis powers. But even before the war began one Japanese diplomat helped save thousands of Jewish refugees.

In November 1939 Japanese diplomat Chiune Sugihara was sent to Lithuania to become the Japanese consul. In the summer of 1940 all foreign diplomats were ordered out of the country. As Sugihara prepared to leave, a delegation of Lithuanian Jews approached. Considering the deteriorating conditions in Europe and fearful of a German invasion of their country, they implored him to issue transit visas so they could immigrate to safety. Stirred by the Jews' plight, Sugihara asked his government for permission to issue the visas. When permission was denied, Sugihara had to make a difficult decision. "For two whole nights," he recalls in his memoir, "[I] was unable to sleep. I eventually decided to issue transit visas. . . . I could not allow these people to die, people who had come to me for help with death staring them in the eyes."

Sugihara began supplying illegal visas to all who asked. Despite repeated warnings from Tokyo, Sugihara managed to issue some thirty-five hundred transit visas before his consulate was shut down. For his role in saving the Lithuanian Jews, Sugihara was recognized as Righteous Among the Nations in 1984.

Quoted in Mordecai Paldiel, *The Righteous Among the Nations*. Jerusalem: Yad Vashem; New York: HarperCollins, 2007, p. 449.

Some six hundred Jews were already safe in Sweden by October 2. After one week, about forty-five hundred refugees had been transported across the strait. By the end of the three-week operation the Danish underground, with the selfless cooperation of the Danish people, had facilitated the rescue of about seventy-two hundred Jews.

Recognizing that the rescue of Danish Jews was a cooperative effort, the members of the Danish Underground requested that Yad

Vashem acknowledge them as a group. A tree was planted along the Avenue of the Righteous at the museum to honor the underground for its part in saving ninety-five percent of Denmark's Jews—a remarkable accomplishment unmatched during the Holocaust.

Innumerable Acts of Resistance

When Adolf Hitler created the Third Reich, he believed his empire would last a thousand years. To achieve his goal he built a formidable army that rapidly took control of Europe. Any opposition to Hitler's empire was swiftly and ruthlessly crushed. It would have been understandable for the millions under Nazi occupation to simply give up. But resistance undertaken by Jews, who made incredible sacrifices under the worst conditions imaginable, and the selfless actions of countless gentiles in hiding and rescuing Jews ultimately helped defeat Hitler's war machine.

"The Jews arrived by train and car, carrying heavy suitcases and small children in their arms, and piled into the boats that were waiting for them with their engines running."[59]

—Jørgen Gersfelt, rescuer of Danish Jews.

The Thousand Year Reich, Hitler's twisted obsession, lasted only twelve years. But the cost was enormous; the lives of six million Jews brutally snuffed out. Without the innumerable acts of armed and spiritual resistance against the Nazis, that cost would have been even higher.

SOURCE NOTES

Introduction: The Myth of Passivity

1. Quoted in Primo Levi, *The Drowned and the Saved*. New York: Vintage, 1989, p. 157.
2. Quoted in Martin Gilbert, *The Holocaust: A History of the Jews of Europe During the Second World War*. New York: Holt, Rinehart and Winston, 1985, p. 368.
3. Quoted in Pesach Schindler, *Hasidic Responses to the Holocaust in the Light of Hasidic Thought*. Hoboken, NJ: Ktav, 1990, p. 64.
4. Raul Hilberg, *The Destruction of the European Jews*. Chicago: Quadrangle, 1961, p. 667.
5. Bruno Bettelheim, foreword to *Auschwitz: A Doctor's Eyewitness Account* by Miklos Nyiszli. New York: Arcade, 2011, p. vii.
6. Nechama Tec, *Defiance*. Oxford: Oxford University Press, 2009, p. xiii.

Chapter One: Fighting Back

7. Quoted in Gunnar S. Paulsson, *Secret City: The Hidden Jews of Warsaw, 1940–1945*. New Haven, CT: Yale University, 2002, p. 73.
8. Quoted in *Jutrznia* (Dawn), "Call to Armed Self-Defense, from an Underground Publication," March 28, 1942. www.yadvashem .org.
9. Quoted in Moshe Arens, *Flags over the Warsaw Ghetto: The Untold Story of the Warsaw Ghetto Uprising*. Jerusalem: Gefen, 2011, p. 318.
10. Quoted in Ber Mark, "The Warsaw Ghetto Uprising," in *They Fought Back: The Story of the Jewish Resistance in Nazi Europe*, ed. Yuri Suhl. New York: Schocken, 1967, p. 107.
11. Quoted in Mark, "The Warsaw Ghetto Uprising," pp. 107–108.
12. Quoted in Mark, "The Warsaw Ghetto Uprising," pp. 113–114.
13. Quoted in Mark, "The Warsaw Ghetto Uprising," p. 119.
14. Quoted in Sara Bender, *The Jews of Bialystok During World War II and the Holocaust*. Waltham, MA: Brandeis University Press, 2008, p. 208.
15. Quoted in Reuben Ainsztein, "The Bialystok Ghetto Revolt," *They Fought Back*, ed. Yuri Suhl, p. 142.

16. Quoted in Bender, *The Jews of Bialystok During World War II and the Holocaust*, p. 259.

17. Quoted in Yankel Wiernik, "A Year in Treblinka," American Representation of the General Jewish Workers' Union of Poland. www.zchor.org.

18. Quoted in Auschwitz.org, "70th Anniversary of the Sonderkommando Revolt." www.auschwitz.org.

19. Quoted in Suhl, introduction to *They Fought Back*, p. 6.

Chapter Two: Spiritual Resistance

20. Quoted in Jennifer Weed, "Beauty and Sadness: Experiencing Poland's History and Jewish Heritage," in *History in the Making*, vol. 5. San Bernardino, CA: Alpha Delta Nu Chapter, Phi Alpha Theta National History Honor Society, University of California at San Bernardino History Department, 2012, p. 21.

21. Quoted in Yisrael Gutman and Michael Berenbaum, eds., *Anatomy of the Auschwitz Death Camp*. Bloomington: Indiana University Press, 1998, p. 525.

22. Abraham Lewin, "Eclipse of the Sun—Universal Blackness. Extracts from the Diary of Abraham Lewin, Warsaw Ghetto—July–September, 1942." www.holocaustresearchproject.org.

23. Lucy Dawidowicz, *The War Against the Jews—1933–1945*. New York: Holt, Rinehart and Winston, 1975, p. 251.

24. Alice Lok, in "Introduction to the Holocaust," United States Holocaust Memorial Museum. www.ushmm.org.

25. Quoted in Doreen Rappaport, "Keeping One's Faith: A Conversation Between Author Doreen Rappaport and Holocaust Survivor Israel Cohen." www.doreenrappaport.com.

26. Quoted in Toby Axelrod, *In the Camps: Teens Who Survived the Nazi Concentration Camps*. New York: Rosen, 1999, p. 25.

27. Quoted in Eve Nussbaum Soumerai and Carol D. Schulz, eds., *Daily Life During the Holocaust*. Westport, CT: Greenwood, 1998, pp. 96–97.

28. Quoted in Lenore J. Weitzman, "Kashariyot (Couriers) in the Jewish Resistance During the Holocaust," Jewish Women's Archive. www.jwa.org.

29. Quoted in Jewish Virtual Library, "Holocaust Resistance: Jewish Resistance to the Nazi Genocide." www.jewishvirtuallibrary.org.

30. Quoted in Ed Vuliami, "Terezín: Music from a Nazi Ghetto," *Guardian*, June 12, 2010. www.theguardian.com.
31. Quoted in Miriam Novitch, Lucy Dawidowicz, and Tom L. Freudenheim, *Spiritual Resistance: Art from Concentration Camps, 1940–1945*. Philadelphia: Jewish Publication Society of America, 1981, p. 17.
32. Gilbert, *The Holocaust*, p. 828.

Chapter Three: The Jewish Partisans

33. Quoted in Holocaust Survivors, "The First Call: Manifesto of Jewish Resistance by Abba Kovner." www.holocaustsurvivors.org.
34. Quoted in Allan Levine, *Fugitives of the Forest: The Heroic Story of Jewish Resistance and Survival During the Second World War*. Guilford, CT: Lyons, 2009, p. 296.
35. Rich Cohen, *The Avengers: A Jewish War Story*. New York: Knopf, 2000, p. 130.
36. Quoted in Cohen, *The Avengers*, p. 155.
37. Quoted in Jewish Partisan Educational Foundation, "Study Guide: Tuvia Bielski: Rescue Is Resistance." www.jewishparti sans.org.
38. Quoted in Peter Duffy, *The Bielski Brothers*. New York: Harper-Collins, 2003, p. 100.
39. Quoted in Duffy, *The Bielski Brothers*, p. 160.
40. Quoted in Duffy, *The Bielski Brothers*, p. x.
41. Quoted in Michael R. Marrus, ed., *The Nazi Holocaust: Historical Articles on the Destruction of European Jews*. Vol. 7: *Jewish Resistance to the Holocaust*. Westport, CT: Meckler, 1989, p. 224.

Chapter Four: Saving the Children

42. Quoted in Rafael Medoff, "Reexamining FDR's Response to Kristallnacht," *Tablet*, November 4, 2014. www.tabletmag.com.
43. Quoted in Holocaust Education and Archive Research Team, "The Kindertransports." www.holocaustresearchproject.org.
44. Quoted in Mark Jonathan Harris and Deborah Oppenheimer, *Into the Arms of Strangers: Stories of the Kindertransport*. New York: Bloomsbury, 2000, p. 107.

45. Quoted in Harris and Oppenheimer, *Into the Arms of Strangers*, p. 123.
46. Quoted in Deborah Durland DeSaix and Karen Gray Ruelle, *Hidden on the Mountain: Stories of Children Sheltered from the Nazis in Le Chambon*. New York: Holiday House, 2007, pp. 118–19.
47. Quoted in Marilyn J. Harran and John Roth, "The Village That Cared," in *The Holocaust Chronicle*. Lincolnwood, IL: Publications International, 2000, p. 510.
48. Quoted in Adam Easton, "Holocaust Heroine's Survival Tale," BBC News, March 3, 2005. www.bbc.co.uk.

Chapter Five: The Righteous Among the Nations

49. Jerusalem Talmud, Sanhedrin 4:1 (22a).
50. Moshe Bejski, "The Righteous Among the Nations and Their Part in the Rescue of Jews," Shoah Resource Center. www.yad vashem.org.
51. Oskar Schindler, "Farewell Address to Jewish Factory Workers at Brünnlitz. Delivered 7 May 1945," American Rhetoric Online Speech Bank. www.americanrhetoric.com.
52. Quoted in Lest We Forget, "Oscar Schindler: Generations Will Remember." www.auschwitz.dk.
53. Quoted in Miep Gies and Alison Leslie Gold, *Anne Frank Remembered: The Story of the Woman Who Helped to Hide the Frank Family*. New York: Simon & Schuster, 2009, p. 88.
54. Gies and Gold, *Anne Frank Remembered*, p. 111.
55. Gies and Gold, *Anne Frank Remembered*, p. 121.
56. Gies and Gold, *Anne Frank Remembered*, pp. 198, 199.
57. Gies and Gold, *Anne Frank Remembered*, p. 11.
58. Leni Yahil, *The Rescue of Danish Jewry: Test of a Democracy*. Philadelphia: Jewish Publication Society of America, 1983, p. 188.
59. Quoted in Mordecai Paldiel, *The Righteous Among the Nations*. Jerusalem: Yad Vashem; New York: HarperCollins, 2007, p. 471.

IMPORTANT PEOPLE

Mordecai Anielewicz

An activist and leader of the Jewish youth underground. Anielewicz was the commander of the Jewish Fighting Organization (ZOB) and fought to his death in the Warsaw ghetto uprising.

Tuvia Bielski

Along with his brothers Asael and Zus, Bielski founded a large partisan fighting unit in the Naliboki Forest in Belarus. He was the leader of the Bielski Partisans, who staged countless sabotage raids on German supply lines and provided a refuge for twelve hundred Jews.

Marceli Galewski

Commander of the underground at the Treblinka concentration camp. After a successful start to an uprising in 1943 camp guards put down the rebellion, and Galewski committed suicide.

Miep Gies

For two years Gies helped hide Jewish teenager Anne Frank and her family in a building annex in Amsterdam, the Netherlands. After the Franks' capture Gies safeguarded Anne's diary, which became a classic part of Holocaust literature.

Abba Kovner

Underground leader in the Vilna ghetto. Kovner wrote a manifesto urging resistance against the Nazi genocide and helped found one of the first armed resistance groups in a Holocaust ghetto. After the war Kovner worked with a secret group to take revenge on former Nazis.

Emanuel Ringelblum

Jewish social activist who kept a personal diary of the Warsaw ghetto and created *Oneg Shabbat*, an archive of documents detailing the Nazi atrocities of the Holocaust.

Oskar Schindler

Businessman and Nazi spy who created a list of his Jewish factory workers who, he told the Nazis, were essential employees. The list, later made famous in a novel and film, saved eleven hundred Jews from deportation to extermination camps.

Irena Sendler

Known as the "Angel of Warsaw," Sendler, acting undercover, rescued some twenty-five hundred Jewish children from the Warsaw ghetto. Her hidden list of children's names helped Sendler reunite some with their families after the war.

Mordechai Tenenbaum

An activist who, under the assumed name "Jozef Tamaroff," gathered information on Nazi activities and helped organize resistance movements in the ghettos. Tenenbaum fought the Nazis during the 1943 liquidation of the Bialystok ghetto.

André Trocmé

Pastor of the protestant church in the French village of Le Chambon-sur-Lignon, Trocmé inspired his congregation and the other residents of the area to provide a safe haven for persecuted Jews seeking refuge. As many as five thousand Jews, mostly children, were saved.

Books

Mary Berg, *The Diary of Mary Berg: Growing Up in the Warsaw Ghetto*. Oxford: Oneworld, 2009.

Rich Cohen, *The Avengers: A Jewish War Story*. New York: Knopf, 2001.

Elaine Saphier Fox, ed., *Out of Chaos: Hidden Children Remember the Holocaust*. Evanston, IL: Northwestern University Press, 2013.

Benjamin Ginsberg, *How the Jews Defeated Hitler: Exploding the Myth of Jewish Passivity in the Face of Nazism*. Lanham, MD: Rowman & Littlefield, 2013.

Deborah Hodge, *Rescuing the Children: The Story of the Kindertransport*. Plattsburgh, NY: Tundra, 2012.

Leon Leyson, *The Boy on the Wooden Box: How the Impossible Became Possible . . . on Schindler's List*. New York: Atheneum, 2013.

Mordecai Paldiel, *The Righteous Among the Nations: Rescuers of Jews During the Holocaust*. New York: HarperCollins, 2007.

Marcel Prins and Peter Henk Steenhuis, *Hidden Like Anne Frank: 14 True Stories of Survival*. New York: Arthur A. Levine, 2011.

Doreen Rappaport, *Beyond Courage: The Untold Story of Jewish Resistance During the Holocaust*. Somerville, MA: Candlewick, 2012.

Internet Sources

Eli Barnavi, "Resistance in the Holocaust." http://www.myjewish learning.com/history/Modern_History/1914-1948/The_Holocaust /War/Resistance.shtml.

Stephen Charles Feinstein, "Holocaust: Art and the Holocaust." www.yivoencyclopedia.org/article.aspx/Holocaust/Art_and_the _Holocaust.

Gary M. Grobman, "Resisters, Rescuers, and Bystanders." www.re member.org/guide/wit.root.wit.res.html.

Websites

Holocaust Survivors (www.holocaustsurvivors.org). Features stories of people who survived the Holocaust, using written accounts, photographs, and audio recordings. Also includes links to Holocaust-related websites and an encyclopedia of Holocaust information.

Jewish Partisan Educational Foundation (www.jewishpartisans. org). A comprehensive website that explores the accomplishments of the Jewish partisans who operated during World War II. Features biographies, interactive maps, photographs, video documentaries, and allows visitors to e-mail a question to a former partisan.

Museum of Tolerance (www.museumoftolerance.com). This website's "Children of the Holocaust" page presents photographs and biographies of more than 120 children who were caught up in the horrors of the Holocaust.

US Holocaust Memorial Museum (www.ushmm.org). A comprehensive guide to the Holocaust, including articles, photographs, films, survivor accounts, and information about the museum in Washington, DC.

Yad Vashem (www.yadvashem.org). Contains a list of non-Jews honored as Righteous Among the Nations since 1963. Among many other features are a searchable database of Holocaust victims, a photo archive, and a resource center with in-depth information about the Holocaust.

INDEX